Real Good Church

How our church came back from the dead, and yours can, too

Rev. Molly Phinney Baskette

Dedication

To my real good church, First Church Somerville:
the best congregation and colleagues a parson could ask for.
To my real great family, Peter, Rafael and Carmen, for keeping
it real and making me happy every day.

The Pilgrim Press
700 Prospect Avenue, Cleveland, Ohio 44115
thepilgrimpress.com

Cover design by Steve McFarland

Illustration by Tuesday Bassen

Printed in the United States of America

First edition: June 2014

10 9 8 7 6 5 4 3 2 1

ISBN 978-0-8298-2002-7

REAL GOOD CHURCH

CONTENTS

Preface

• • •

I field-tested the ideas in this book on a group of pastors from Kansas and Oklahoma who were ready to revitalize their churches. While they were enthusiastic and receptive, I also heard: "What if my church is not anywhere near ready to do any of this stuff? I can't seem to get them unstuck from where they are. They're just so afraid of change."

This is what I told them: my new favorite definition of leadership is from Ron Heifetz: "Leadership is disappointing people at a rate they can tolerate."

And sometimes, at a rate they cannot tolerate. When you begin to do this work, people will become unhappy, and some of them will leave. This is to be expected, and it is OK. There are plenty of churches out there for people who want things to stay exactly the same, for people who hate disruption and innovation, for people who are committed to the idea of God-approved homophobia, among other things.

What there aren't enough of is churches that are open, welcoming, flexible, playful, and forward-moving.

Often in churches we are stationed at the back door, anxious about and attending to one or two or a few people who have decided to leave, and nobody's paying any attention to the front door, where (perhaps many) people just coming in are looking for orientation and nurturing assimilation. Don't privilege the people who have been at your church over the people outside your community who don't even know about you yet—these are *all* God's people, and if you are a pastor you took vows to "minister impartially to the needs of all."

Your work, as a pastor or lay leader, is to build up your own tolerance for disappointing people. Learn how to evaluate criticism for what it can teach you, don't take it personally, and don't let it slow you down or hijack God's work.

Most importantly, when you're beginning this work, look for allies. I don't mean friends in the congregation, "yes" men and women, but individuals in the congregation who have personal authority and charisma, who have the ear of the congregation. They may be young, but they may not. They will probably be extroverts, or fake it well.

One of my best allies at First Church Somerville was an octogenarian named Dick. There were three things he would say over and over again, that acted like water over the great immoveable rock of a dying mainline church.

1. During the process of becoming open to and affirming of LGBT people, Dick (a retired cop) would tell a story of a cop he used to work with who loved to hunt, would always bring him some venison, and happened to be gay—in the 70s. "He was a bang-up guy," Dick would say.
2. When Dick talked about our church's welcome, he would remember when he himself was a young man of 20, Episcopalian, and his Scottish Congregational fiancée made him promise as a condition of marrying him that he would start coming to our church instead. "The men of this congregation made me feel so welcome," he would say. And cry. Every time. This was a man who understood what it meant to be welcomed

for his own sake. He reminded me that not every old-timer in the congregation was *always* an old-timer. We can ask individuals in our church to remember when and how they entered the community, what it felt like.

3. Of the leadership of our young people, Dick would say, "Those of us who used to run everything in the church are getting old. We're tired. We have to get out of the way and let the young people lead. And that doesn't mean they're going to do it our way. We have to give them permission to do it their way."

People listened to Dick. He quieted (some of) the anxiety—enough to begin to leverage change. Hopefully you have someone like Dick in your congregation—a natural leader who can articulate what is good and hopeful about change. The vision and goals shouldn't all be coming from one person in the church. This is deeply shared work, and the more we share it—remind our congregations of what they say they want, to grow—the less likely it is that the enterprise will devolve into a personality conflict between a single person and a vocal opposition, with a silent majority standing by, anxious and afraid to speak up.

Another issue that came up among the pastors in Kansas and Oklahoma was the latent jealousy some long-termers have for the newbies, who get the pastor's main attention at coffee hour. This is where office hours come in handy. My people know I am available to them every single week, and by appointment. There is even a running joke in my church that when I stop talking to you at coffee hour, that's a good thing—it means you've "arrived," you're an insider. I have carefully cultivated a culture of "newbies first at coffee hour," *and* my people know that if they really need me, I will be there for them—but they have to ask.

Remember that besides your allies in the church, your best resource is a non-anxious presence. Don't come to a church council meeting with your voice high and tight, your body language aggressive or passive, with a 10-page white paper for Why This Thing Needs To Be Changed Immediately.

All those things communicate defensiveness and rigidity to your people. Even if you don't feel relaxed, fake it. Talk to your spiritual director, friends outside the church, pray a lot to prepare yourself. Then, when you come with an idea, be clear and compelling but also casual, informal. I'll often say something like, "I have this crazy idea—help me make it better. I'd like to try this once/for six weeks/for six months and if it doesn't work we don't have to do it anymore." Because I've said the C word myself, I've stolen its power—and more often than not, I get permission (and, they really do make my ideas better!).

Finally, if your church is really stuck, consider that you haven't articulated the Doomsday scenario sufficiently. Enlist their self-interest in concrete ways. It was when we said out loud to each other, "At our current rate of spending we have about four years of money left" that we really got moving. We didn't say "In four years we can sell the parsonage and keep limping along for ten more years." We didn't do half-measures. The old people understood that if they didn't get on board, they might not have a church to be buried from. It was a powerful motivation to give permission for change.

Doom, Gloom, and a Kernel of Hope

• • •

I pastor a gorgeous, eclectic, young, *hilarious,* vibrant, urban, frustratingly transient progressive Christian church. Though the reality on the inside is a little more nuanced, others have held us up as a model of renewal and "how to do church" here at the end of the Christian empire, when so many churches have seen the writing on the wall.

Ten years ago, we were in the same spot as those churches. We had done the math, and we knew something had to change, or we would die. We had about 35 people in worship, on average. Many of them were elderly, and have since passed away. We had about $200,000 in the bank, and we owned our building, as well as a parsonage, but New England is one of the most expensive areas of the country, and what we had wouldn't go far if we stayed in our financial and numerical nosedive.

This manual will break down all the measures we took to get into the position we are in today. Our current worship attendance averages 130 (even in the summer!), with 350 on Easter—which for urban New England is practically a megachurch. Our giving has more than quintupled in the last decade. When I arrived as pastor in 2003, we had six children in our Sunday school program, and today we have close to 100.

We passed a lot of risky budgets—visionary budgets—over these last 10 years, and last year, for the first time, we passed our first balanced budget. We did this less than a year after we raised $600,000 in a capital improvement campaign to fix our crumbling building.

There are lots of other more subtle signs of spiritual renewal, which I'll tell you about as we go along, but I wanted you to know up front that our renewal has credibility, so you'll buy in. I know how pastors can spin the renewal talk, when the factual reality is otherwise (I've done it myself! Fake it till ya make it.)

I've also read everything, and know that in the bibliography of church renewal, there's a lot of plain old junk, and there's also a lot of stuff that is great but falls under the category of what I call "swirly talk." That is, it provides a great theological rationale, but it doesn't tell you What To Do.

I'm not going to tell you what to do, but I will tell you what *we* did, and let you, who know your communities best, decide what applies. I'm writing this manual because our church is alive and well, *and* yours can be, too. Our demographics may be different from yours, our leaders are different, but many of the things we did to survive and thrive can be replicated in any church, anywhere.

I will say that even though our church is pretty different demographically from most other churches out there, much of what we did is not based on the fact that we are young, or progressive, or urban, or live in a city that was just named one of the hippest in America, albeit by a non-accredited source.

The people in our church are human, and we function like all humans (skinny jeans and piercings notwithstanding). We are humans who believe in God, or want to believe in God more. We want to be a good church and a *real* church, a church where the truth gets told and to which we can bring our whole selves. A church where when we worship together we leave it all on the field. A church where we can laugh all of our laughter and cry all of our tears and ask the hardest questions and feel that the Holy Spirit shows up with great regularity, because the hairs on the back of our necks go up or we start to cry. A church where when we show up we get the courage or wisdom we need to make changes in our lives.

But now I've started with the "swirly talk"! and I want to keep this practical. Because, let's be honest: we don't have any time to waste.

WHAT WE'RE UP AGAINST

You've read all the same articles I have about the decline of the mainline church, the rise of the Nones (people raised without any organized religion), and the end of Christianity as we know it. Great! Churches have died, are dying, will die. But that doesn't mean that they *all* will.

Some of our churches will make it. The reality is, we're not losing people to demographic changes. We're losing them to bad messaging, and to brunch—at least in my neighborhood. Christianity has committed the sin of being hateful and violent (I won't trot out the whole list, but it starts with Constantine and ends with Fred Phelps). Nearly as bad, it has committed the sin of being boring and fake. I'm not going to bash the Church anymore—that's what Facebook is for. We have work to do!

People ask me a lot: what one thing made a difference in turning your church around? I answer: We didn't do one thing. We did a lot of things. This manual will tell you exactly what we did, and how we did it. Not all of these things will work in your setting and culture—but lots of them will.

That's good news. It doesn't take freakily charismatic leadership or a superbly gifted preacher or a once-in-a-lifetime windfall to make this happen. One of the leaders in our church called our renewal "a gift from God that we worked really hard to be able to receive."

I've learned a lot along the way—that is, I stole a lot from other smart, hardworking pastors and lay leaders and church growth coaches.

But it all belongs to the Holy Spirit, doesn't it? So we want to pass it on to you. Because we believe that while brunch is good, what real, good church can offer us is so much better.

In case you've forgotten why you do this thing called church, and how to articulate it to others who don't know about it yet, here's a great list from the awesome Rev. Anne Russ of Argenta Presbyterian. (See? Stolen!)

> ***Ten Reasons Why You Should Be Going to Church***
>
> I've just seen one too many articles on why people aren't coming to church. Admittedly, there are some good reasons. But I'd like to share my top 10 reasons why you *should* be coming to church. Others will have different reasons and some may disagree with the ones I have listed, but here they are.
>
> 10. Coming to church doesn't mean you have no doubts about God or faith or religion. It means you have a place you can share with people who have their own doubts.
> 9. Bad stuff is going to happen in your life. It just is. A church community cannot be everything to everyone in times of crisis, but when the bottom falls out of your world, it's great to have a community to lift you back up.
> 8. Bad stuff is going to happen in your life, part two. The time to build a relationship with God is not when life turns ugly, and you've run out of all other options. Attending worship regularly helps build a relationship with God and others that will give you a solid foundation when the winds blow and the storms come.
> 7. Not all churches are anti-something. Most of us are for people, for acceptance, for hospitality. Really, we're out there. We just don't get the good press.
> 6. Any church worth its salt has really good food on a regular basis.
> 5. Churches offer paint-by-number opportunities to serve. Many

people would like to help the poor, the hungry and the homeless, but they don't know how to get involved, how to make the time to be involved, or what they can do to really make a difference. Churches offer you ways to plug in to help those who need it most.

4. You've got a gift. Probably two or ten of them. Becoming involved in the ministry of a church will help you discover and use gifts you never even knew you had.
3. Not all churches are after your money. Good churches want you to have a healthy relationship with money. Sure, churches need to pay the electric bill and the pastor and the youth director, but money and the church is more about you than it is about the church. It's about your own relationship with money. World events have proven that it's much better to put faith in God than in a bank account. Church can help you with that.
2. Taking a break from our hectic lives to come to church is accepting the gift of Sabbath. Wayne Mueller says "[Sabbath] dissolves the artificial urgency of our days, because it liberates us from the need to be finished." We don't take Sabbath and come to worship because we have time and have finished up everything that needs to be done. We take Sabbath because it is time to stop, and we are designed to stop, rest and reflect. Those who don't are destined to crash and burn.
1. Jesus is really cool. Even if you don't know if you can believe in the whole Son-of-God thing, even if you refer to the resurrection as the Zombie Jesus event and even though those of us already in church often do a lousy job of following him, come to church to get to know Jesus. The more you get to know him, the more you'll understand why people call his way The Way.

Rev. Anne Russ, Pastor, Argenta Presbyterian Church,
North Little Rock, Arkansas

And: even though I've exhausted my list of things to talk about, I know this manual is far from done. *Write to me* and tell me what your church does well that we don't, or that we've forgotten about. Tell me what I left out!

THE DANGER WE ARE IN

I was in a supervision meeting with our student minister last year, and found myself saying for the hundredth time: "I am preparing you to lead a dying church, because the reality is, all of our churches are dying. It may be dying quickly or it may be dying slowly, but it's sure 'nuff dying. Even if it *was* growing under the previous pastor, the congregation is in a new time of uncertainty because that pastor has left, and they're not sure *they* can keep up the growth. So, it's up to you to lead them, and convince them, by casting the right vision, setting the right priorities, and inspiring them to the right changes."

It's an old saw that seminary doesn't really prepare you to lead a church. I loved my seminary experience but I still had to learn a lot of things on the job. Until the core curriculum in mainline Protestant seminaries changes significantly, you will have to have a good field placement, read lots of books, attend churches that are *working,* and take lots of notes.

When I was working with the church growth consultants Paul Nickerson and Jim Griffiths back in 2005, they said that in 20 years, all the unhealthy churches would be dead. They will have run out of money and out of people, and only the churches that had figured out relevancy and authenticity and healthy communication would be left.

I liked this idea at the time: it was so clean and winnowing, an echo of Matthew 3:12: "His winnowing fork is in his hand, and he will clear his threshing floor, gathering his wheat into the barn and burning up the chaff with unquenchable fire."

It was also a great comfort to the part of me that loves things tidy and clean. People wouldn't have to risk walking into a mean church, or a desperate church, because all of us left would be kind, truly welcoming and God-positive. That is, we would be hungry for people for their own sakes, and not because we wanted their money or their bottoms in the pews (which people can *always* sense, by the way).

About a year ago, I had an epiphany. I think it's from God, but only time will tell, won't it? Here it is: I'm thinking that not only, say, a tenth of our churches, but something more like 80% of our mainline Christian churches will be dead. And they don't even know it yet. There is something ineffably sad about this idea. It's like staring at a sky full of stars, only some of those stars don't know the truth: though we can still see their light, they're already gone.

This means time is short. A parishioner at the first church I served as an ordained minister gave me a Beanie Baby snail, symbolic of how slow the church moves when it has decisions to make. We as leaders have to create a sense of urgency around renewal and change, or it will be too late for some of us. We don't have time to make sure every single person in our congregation feels totally OK about proposed changes, because that's never going to happen—some people are just congenitally risk-averse, and they will hold the church hostage to their commitment to the *status quo.* Until there's no church left.

DOOMSDAY POLLYANNA

I've invented a little character I call the Doomsday Pollyanna. Clergy and lay leaders do well to play this part in our churches: communicating the urgency of doing things well and/or differently to our people, while also communicating how confident we are that we *can* do it. Whether the issue is money, or space, or changes to liturgy, or widening our welcome—you have to be clear with people that what's at stake is the death of the church for *everybody,* and what's possible is: the life of the church, for everybody already there who buys into the vision, as well as many more people who aren't aware that this place and people are going to become an important part of their lives.

An important function of Doomsday Pollyanna is managing the public message: knowing how to cast the vision, reach for low-hanging fruit, and celebrate every win so that the people's confidence in themselves and faith in God's work among them is secured. At the same time, the Doomsday Pollyanna needs to calibrate expectations—to seize on the natural anxiety that is always washing through the congregation, to titrate it to manageable levels, and then *use* it. Remember: urgency, and optimism, simultaneously.

Let me be clear: you can't do everything at once. Don't try to, or you will burn out or exhaust your people. Do what you can, when you can. Look for the next opening God is giving you, and move into it. Pray a lot, and do a lot of checking in with your most trusted leaders about priorities.

That said, IMHO your average dying church will probably have to address pretty much every issue in this book, sooner or later.

WHO I AM: ONE PASTOR

I am a working mom in my mid-40s. I got ordained when I was 28, after graduating seminary and spending a year living in voluntary poverty at a Mexican orphanage, with my then-bf/now hubby. We've got two kids, ages 7 and 12, who, thank God, love church, or it would be harder than it is to serve one!

My first call was to a fairly typical large suburban church. I was the full-time associate pastor, but had the blessing/curse/windfall to serve at a time when the longtime senior minister was leaving. They didn't find an interim right away, and so three months after I arrived, I found myself the sole pastoral staff person (and functional C.E. director) of a 500-person church, from Christmas Eve until Maundy Thursday. This meant I lucked into a lot of authority and opportunity, early on (and also a 70-hour work week!).

I moved to my current church about ten years ago. More on them below. I started as a three-quarter time solo pastor, and as the church has grown, I've remained three-quarter time—we've grown the staff rather than my hours, which is how I want it. There are a lot of (adult) preacher's kids in my congregation, and I've learned from them how hard it was to grow up playing second fiddle to the church's needs and demands. The church can be a big, demanding baby if we let it, and I want my kids to know that they come first—not every single time, but overall. These are my kids after all—I chose to have them, and *they* are my primary responsibility, not the church.

As a dear friend of mine says, the vows we make in marriage and the vows we make in baptism are what *allow* us to keep our ordination vows. That is, when we nurture those relationships closest to us, they juice us for pastoring, and we become better ministers.

WHO WE ARE: OUR CHURCH

Our official denomination is the United Church of Christ (UCC), Congregational flavor. Our spiritual ancestors are the Pilgrims and the Puritans. They joined forces, mellowed out, and became the Congregationalists, who in turn joined forces with the Evangelical & Reform tradition back in 1957. We are a small but mighty, mostly progressive, and democratically governed denomination of just under a million members. Barack Obama was UCC when he was a community organizer, and later a lawyer, in Chicago.

First Church Somerville UCC, my parish, is located in the metro Boston area. We're surrounded by colleges and universities, and the median age of our city is 31. It is a very young city, very liberal, and very skeptical, religiously speaking. Most of the self-identified religious residents are older Portuguese, Brazilian, and Italian Catholics, or new Brazilian, Haitian, or Central American evangelicals. Demographic data suggests that, at any given time, only 3% of the population is unchurched *and* interested in finding a church. Keeping a mainline (read: largely Anglo) Protestant church going here is hard work.

Back in the day, there were at least five Congregational churches in my dense city of 68,000. They were all strong. My own church boasted 1,000 members in the 1940s. Then white flight from the urban centers began to draw mainliners out into the burbs. The growing failure of confidence in institutions like the organized church, fed by the Vietnam War and the winds of social change, began to polish off the downtown churches. Now we are the last Congregational church left. All of the others merged with ours, or quietly died.

When I came to First Church Somerville in 2003, there was an average of about 35 people in worship. They were mostly white, many over 70, but with a strong contingent of younger adults ages 20-50, who were willing to work hard to listen to God and do whatever it took to resurrect their church.

When I arrived, they had already done the hard work of going through the Open and Affirming (ONA) process: an educational and emotional process in which a local church in the United Church of Christ explores the Christian theology of sexual orientation; other denoms have a similar process, with a name of their own creation. At the end of the process, the congregation takes a vote, and, God willing, results in the unanimous or near-unanimous expression of full welcome of LGBT folks into the life and leadership of the church. First Church took such a vote in 1999.

But by 2003, when I arrived, they hadn't really begun to harvest the blessing of their courageous decision. There was no visibly public indication of this welcome, only a little coded language on the outdoor sign, and a brief description on the church's website. One of the first things we did was make that welcome explicit and unapologetic, and it has made all the difference.

I'm not saying everyone needs to go through such a process to thrive, although I do think it is the holy, faithful and loving thing to do (more on that later). But it is the single biggest contributing factor to why we are alive today.

Today, First Church has about 125-175 in worship on an ordinary Sunday, which makes our sanctuary feel pleasantly full. Easter and Christmas have become crowd-control affairs, topping 300 people.

We match our neighborhood. We skew young (70% of our current attendees are under 40; only 1% of them are over 70). We skew queer: 40% of our attendees are LGBT-identified. We skew liberal: we have a drag-queen-in-residence. When we were searching for an associate pastor last year, this is how we described ourselves:

"We're not your parents' church, but we're the church you'll bring your parents to."

This mix of folks makes doing church wicked fun, as we say in Boston. Unfortunately, most folks don't make Boston their final destination: our people are living through major transitions, running hard after education, careers, significant relationships, all of which have the power to move them on geographically after only a couple years. Every year, we say goodbye to at least 15% of our population: our First Church Diaspora, as we call them.

The silver lining is: nobody says, "We've never done it that way before," because we change so fast, there is no single way we have ever done anything, in living memory!

WHAT YOU CAN DO WITH 30 GOOD MEMBERS AND A BAD BUILDING

There have been times over the last 10 years that I really despaired of "getting there"—"there" being a place of sustainability, of having a certain amount of positive momentum so that it wouldn't always be so much *work* to grow.

Our church building is 101 years old, and a liability in many ways. It has three stories, but a rabbit warren of staircases and dark tiny ill-used rooms on *seven* different levels, such that it's a nightmare regarding accessibility and plain old viability for multi-purpose ministry or rental space.

It's a tired building: something, usually something expensive, is always breaking. It's just old enough that some things are breaking for the first time, like the horsehair plaster in the sanctuary that has been falling on our heads for a while (although it makes a nice sermon illustration about the temporality of the church).

I remember complaining one time to our church growth consultant, "Oh, what we could do if we had a few more people and didn't have this stupid building!"

He stopped me in my tracks. "I work with new church start pastors every day. They would *kill* for 30 people and a bad building." It's all a matter of perspective.

There is an upside to having so few people. There are fewer sacred cows to kill, fewer leaders to bring on board. It is easier to communicate the vision in depth to every individual. There is a tremendous sense of urgency. People are very motivated to pitch in, and do multiple jobs, even (fortunately or unfortunately) tasks that aren't intuitive to them. And pastors have a lot of influence in small churches: unless there has been a breach of pastoral ethics in the recent or even distant past, there is a high degree of trust and respect for the pastor's vision.

And as for buildings, even a bad building is a building. You don't have to deal with the vagaries of a landlord, setting up chairs, schlepping and storing stuff each week. With a building you have free advertising, all day, every day. You have equity, which you can turn into cash if absolutely necessary: you should in any case be renting out your building to its fullest potential (while making sure you reserve adequate space for your own expanding ministries), and you can mortgage it to enact dramatic turnaround ministry ideas.

READ ME FIRST: THE FIRST THREE MONTHS

If you're a grizzled veteran of parish ministry, you probably have your own list, which may look a lot like mine. But if you've never served a church before and are taking your first call and are wondering where to begin, here's a short list of things I would recommend you concentrate on in your first three months.

1. Meet individually with every single person in your congregation who comes to worship at least once a month, and also with elderly shut-ins, who are an amazing source of lore, including sacred cows. Ask them about themselves—do more listening than talking. Ask them what makes them tick, where they have felt loved and where and when they have experienced the presence of God in their church. Ask them what their hopes and dreams for the future of this community are—and listen for cues that will tell you if they are really open to change or are risk-averse. Learn to love each one of them for their own sake, *and* cultivate allies for change. Not all of them will be instant allies for radical change, and that is OK. Look for the wise, cheerful and healthy leaders whom the others will get behind.
2. Take a serious inventory of the building, its spaces and whether or not they align with the best purposes and potential (e.g. is the Sunday school in a smelly basement room? Are the hallways cluttered? Is the signage terrible?) Be careful what you move or change (see Epic Failures). Prioritize a couple of easy DIY projects to make the building signage more fluent, or to make spaces brighter and more hospitable. Pace yourself, include everybody in the work (especially cheerful people with lots of relationships in the church), and publicly celebrate every project when you're done.
3. Go on neighborhood walks. Shop locally, make friends with the school crossing guards, chat up the guy hanging out on the park bench. Eavesdrop on conversations at coffee shops. Read demographic data—your denomination may have a contract with an outfit like Mission Insite, but you can also get at least some basic data for free online. But there is no substitute for shoe leather and your own eyeballs when it comes to really learning what makes a community tick, and what needs are underserved.

4. Make your sermons *good*. This is your big chance, every week, to set a new course and unleash the energy of your community. Establish your preaching voice, the emerging shared vision, the priorities, the strengths of the congregation. Build the congregation's self-esteem by reflecting back to them the holiness that you see among them. Spend enough time on your sermons that they are sermons worth hearing. Don't be afraid to be funny, or edgy, or vulnerable. Tell lots of stories! Do your sermon homework—there's no substitute for good exegesis—but don't load people down with scholarship and jargon; make it the stock for the sauce. And if you feel nervous putting on that microphone, remember: we preachers are not here to rival the TED talkers and get page views, but to bring the Good News to our own dear people. A friend of mine once reminded me, "The sheep know the sound of the shepherd's voice."

CHAPTER ONE

The Building

• • •

PASSIVE SIGNAGE AND ACTIVE SIGNAGE

Your church building has way more signs than you think it does. The locked front door, the boxes piled up in corners that assault the newcomer's gaze, the messy Sunday school room, the nursery with dangerous or broken toys, the bulletin boards with ancient announcements, the mold growing all over the women's bathroom (yes, that happened at my own church this past very humid summer). All these signs send the message: We're depressed. We're not ready for you. We're not healthy. We don't want you, and we don't understand what your children need *at all*.

One of the first things we focused on after I came to Somerville was signage. We couldn't afford a new sign out front (that took about eight years and $5,000! Those suckers are expensive!), but it was cheap and easy to deal with our passive signage, as well our interior signage (maybe $1,000 for all-new vinyl signs to get people where they needed to go inside the building).

If you've been at your church for a while, you might not see what's not working. Get a friend, preferably someone who is great at being very honest and who has never set foot in your church, to come over. Don't meet them out front—have them find their own way in, with the church how it usually is on a Sunday morning (same doors locked/unlocked).

Have them write down everything they notice, and all the obstacles to entry and to finding their way around easily. I once went to a job interview at a church and had to try four separate exterior doors before I picked the right one! It was humiliating. If it was humiliating for me, who had a definite purpose and invitation to be there, how must it feel to a shy person who has never been to church before and doesn't know if they really are welcome?

Walk around with your friend, once in the building, but let them lead the way. Have them pretend they need to use the bathroom, or they have children to drop off at Sunday school, or they are coming into worship 10 minutes late. Can they easily find what they need? How many decisions/wrong turns do they have to make to find the sanctuary? What do they see along the way? How would they, as a maybe slightly critical newcomer, judge what they see? Is there room for them at the back, in worship, when they sneak in? Is there still someone to hand them a bulletin, if they are ten minutes late? The bulletin itself is a form of passive signage—more on that in the "Bulletin" section.

INTERIOR SIGNAGE

Make sure the signs are easily visible and navigable. Don't use coded language (don't point the way to the "Narthex" or "Sacristy"!). Put up paper signs and arrows for a while, and vet your name and place signage through several other people, to crowdsource the best possible configuration, before you buy your permanent interior signs.

EXTERIOR SIGNAGE

Our church is pretty lucky, because we are on a main thoroughfare that has hundreds of cars and probably close to a thousand pedestrians or bikers move by every single day. More about this in our "Outreach Tabling" section.

But even if you are on a less trafficked street or even a cul-de-sac, your church lot and building are available for all the free advertising you'd like. Within six months, we hung a rainbow flag off our front entry. See the "Open and Affirming" section for more backstory on this. The flag became the number-one identified reason why new people came to church. Almost without exception, when asked, everyone said, "I saw the rainbow flag and I knew it meant you were a welcoming church." The flag and flagpole together cost about $50. We wear out about two flags a year, as they get sun-bleached and tattered. It is a good problem to have.

REPURPOSING SPACE

Make a list of the spaces and issues you need to address to make your church bright and beautiful. You don't need to have a capital campaign to make this happen. Prioritize them, and pick them off one at a time. Our church consultant said: make the women's bathroom nice first, because if a family or a straight couple comes, it's likely the woman who will be the one to decide whether or not they come back.

Our women's bathroom used to be like something from your grandma's ancient cottage in Maine: always a little smelly, peeling paint, broken tiles, rickety toilets, under-functioning door locks. We spent about $1,000 on bright paint, raspberry and royal blue vinyl tile, a new sink and efficient toilets. I put some high-end fragrance sticks in there, and some cheap IKEA art. It made a world of difference! Suddenly, the bathroom was the nicest place in the building. We began to congregate in there at coffee hour. I'm only kidding a little bit.

You only have to renovate one space at a time. That's what we have done. When you renovate or repurpose, renovate to the church you want to be in 2-5 years, not the church you are now. Don't dream small, and outgrow your vision too quickly! It'll be cheaper and more efficient in the long run to dream to the right degree.

NURSERY

When I came to Somerville, we had a long, narrow, little-used chapel that housed about four electric organs people had kindly donated over the years. In one corner, instead of an organ, there was a plastic trash bag full of toys. That was our "nursery." One parent from our two families with young children would stay with the kids (who were much more interested in the organs than the toys) while the others worshipped upstairs. It was dreadful.

We framed and sheetrocked an inexpensive wall to divide the space, and planted a nursery on one side. Cheerful homemade curtains, fresh paint and carpet, a little IKEA storage furniture, donated sofa, good toys, an amateur hand-painted wall mural from Tomie DePaola's *Children's Bible* and *voila!* We had a nursery. On the day we dedicated and blessed it, an 8-months pregnant woman came to church for the first time. She knew we were ready for her. She stayed, and has taken just about every important job in the church, as one of our most gifted and committed leaders.

CHAPEL

On the chapel side of the newly divided area, we knew we wanted to use this space for smaller funerals and summer worship, which was lightly attended at the time. We had nursing mothers, and education was important to our congregation, so we created built-in comfortable seating at the back in a semi-private area, with custom bookshelves for a spiritual reading library. We filled it with plants. Our colors were strong but soothing. We trolled the "as is" table at Home Depot for funky discount lighting. We spent six weeks, every Saturday, with an architect and a carpenter who attend our church and donated their time to make this happen. When it was done, we blessed and dedicated this space as well (celebrate, celebrate, celebrate every win!). The chapel remains, I believe, our biggest source of DIY pride.

OFFICE AND SUNDAY SCHOOL SPACE

We had a stage in our lower parish hall that the kids loved to run on at coffee hour. We never used it for theatrical productions—in fact, we were nesting a theatre company, but they found it so dark and difficult that they built their own temporary stages to use. A previous generation of First Churchers had taped black plastic garbage bags over the windows behind the stage to keep out the light. Backstage was a repository for old junk and mouse nests.

As we grew, we needed a real modern office and a Sunday school room, so we decided to tear up the stage. Under that stage was another, smaller, stage. Under *that* stage was another stage! (That made great sermon fodder: whenever you are making changes like this that might feel "big" to the congregation, preach preach preach, storytell, teach and communicate why you are making these changes so everyone is brought on board and feels like it is a change they had a hand in).

Finally, we got to the subfloor. New walls went up, we put in a long counter in the church office with multiple inviting workstations, plenty of storage (a problem that had dogged us in our 100-year old Victorian building), and a bright, cheerful Sunday school room with glass windows embedded in the wall at children's eye-level between the room and the parish hall, so that sunlight from the exterior windows could shine through into the hall.

We painted a chalkboard on one area of the wall on both the Sunday school room side and the parish hall side, and painted "Beloved Community" high up on the frieze in our now-lemon-and-orange parish hall. We put bright Mexican oilcloths on our banquet tables, much easier to keep clean and more durable than cheap plastic.

This has become our iconic image of the church: Beloved Community, an expression of who we are as well as a mandate for the future, smiling down on tables that invite people to sit and feast on food as well as relationships with one another.

SANCTUARY

Interestingly enough, our sanctuary is coming last in our sequencing of renovations, probably because it is the most expensive. Don't get me wrong, we have done some key things along the way: we built a sound booth so we could have the right equipment to record a podcast; we shortened pews and capped them so that folks in wheelchairs could sit with their friends and family.

We replaced the carpeting, after we noticed that for months one of our aging deacons was coloring in the threadbare spots on the chancel steps with a red Sharpie.

But don't underestimate how motivating it can be to have a careworn sanctuary. I've preached about it a *lot.* First, from the perspective of: Isn't it great we have our priorities straight, that we are investing in the nursery before the sanctuary? And later, from the perspective of: See that hole in the ceiling—what if that's where the Holy Spirit gets in? And now, from the perspective of: We have a beautiful spirit and heart in this church; now are we ready to fund an outer beauty that matches our inner beauty?

There are different theologies for different stages of this renewal journey. It's not that our values change, but our capacity changes. Ask too much of people all at once, and they will feel discouraged and not know how to get where you all want to go. Ask too little, and they will never find out what they are capable of, what Jesus has given them the power to do.

FRONT YARD

We live in a very dense urban area—the densest municipality in New England. We have decent parks but not enough of them, and not enough community garden space to meet the demand. A couple of years ago, we dug up our front lawn, which we couldn't find enough volunteers to mow anyhow, and built a terraced garden. We got a little grant money from an organization in Detroit called Urban Farming, and supplemented with grant money from another source.

For four seasons now, we have had a thriving vegetable garden. We bought a $50 sign from Vistaprint that invites our neighbors to help themselves to cherry tomatoes, peaches, kale and herbs. (They do! Including the local homeless and marginal folk.) We give the bulk of the harvest to our local food bank, and serve some at the coffee hour table. We pay one of our members to plant, weed, water and harvest the garden, because we understand that it is one the most important signs of our health and vitality. The children love to help in the garden during Sunday school, and we always have volunteers to help with the work as well—people without yards who want to get their hands in the dirt. They don't want to mow, but they want to trellis beans!

At the front of the garden we have a prayer garden. There's a park bench, a butt can (we have a lot of homeless folks and addicts who walk up and down the street), a garbage can, and free wireless that reaches into this area. We have had in the past, and will again, a prayer box and notepad, as well as a Twitter account hashtag or email address, to which people can address their prayers for our Prayer Team to pray. We also have a plan to do a Little Free Library (littlefreelibrary.org) with spiritual books it.

ALL CHURCH WORK DAY

We're not lucky enough to have a dedicated sexton who is always at the church fixing or cleaning something, so a practice that predates me at our church, but which I eagerly anticipate, is the All Church Work Day.

It happens once in the spring and once in the fall, on a Sunday after coffee hour, for about three hours. We get a *lot* done. We scrub the kitchen and the fridge, reorganize and throw things away, get whole rooms painted, run the nursery toys through the dishwasher. We take out air conditioners and winterize the building in fall, we plant the garden in the spring and put the air conditioners back in. We've pulled up all the sanctuary carpet, gotten bats and pigeon poop out of the belfry, and in general made all things new—or new-ish.

We group people in new friendship and affinity groups for tasks that suit them, we play fun music in every room, and serve the best pizza in our city to celebrate and reward the volunteers. It's *fun* and it really makes a difference to the mood and look of our church. It's work that honors God and Her house, and gives newbies a sense of ownership as they peer in closets and give up elbow grease to making their new church work better.

CHAPTER TWO

Children's Ministry and Adult Spiritual Formation

• • •

BEAUTIFUL, CLEAN SPACES AND LOW-HANGING FRUIT

I've already talked about the importance of making sure key spaces in the church are clean, warm and welcoming. Bathrooms, nursery and Sunday school classrooms, in that order, are far more important than sanctuary or fellowship hall. They are also smaller and easier to tackle with DIY labor and a few trips to the altars of IKEA or Target.

These are also spaces that kids and volunteers will want to be in if they are pleasant! Look for easy tasks, get them done, take pictures and celebrate, celebrate, celebrate every win.

SAFE CHURCH AND BACKGROUND CHECKS

It probably goes without saying after the major reforms in boundary awareness and safe church training as a response to the clergy sexual abuse crisis in the late 90s, but you simply cannot have a children's ministry/Sunday school program without having a safe church policy.

We have a two-adult rule: two adults present in every classroom and youth group setting, for accountability and support. We also do criminal records checks on all of the church staff, and anyone volunteering with the children's ministry program.

There might still be a few parents out there willing to tolerate a disorganized church without a proactive safe church policy, but they shouldn't be willing to: the stakes are too high, and it's a fact that would-be abusers who choose and groom their victims all too often find churches a favorable place to operate.

PAID PROFESSIONAL CAREGIVERS

We pay our lead Sunday school teachers. You heard me right.

As our church began to grow, we mostly grew with unmarried young adults. Many of them moved away to other God-given pursuits, but some of them stayed. Then they married. Then they started having children. About half of our church children arrived not because their families moved into our city but because they were born into our church.

We never thought we would be a "typical" vibrant church with a big Sunday school, but we were wrong. The problem was, as we grew, what to do with our kids? We didn't have the kind of volunteer resources other churches had: the diehard church members willing to give up four months to a year of worship at a time in order to teach kids (well, we did, but the one person burned out, and you probably have the same problem).

We decided to hire one paid person for each classroom, and add classrooms as our numbers grew to support the cell division. The benefits to hiring Sunday school staff were obvious to us:

- greater consistency for babies and toddlers (and parents!) facing stranger anxiety, leaving their kids with a new person each week in the nursery or classroom
- greater accountability for preparation in the Sunday school classrooms
- higher quality programming and content in the Sunday school program; higher quality of care in the nursery

- less of a burden on church members and friends, who could spend more time in worship, developing their own spiritual life, and reducing burnout factor

You might think there would be a lot of complaining about spending money on teachers, but there isn't. We pay our teachers/nursery staff person about $45 per Sunday. People know that it is cheap money: there is a very high return on that investment. Our teachers get one Sunday off each month, when we worship intergenerationally, since Sunday school normally meets at the same time as worship.

The only downside to hiring children's ministry staff is: it is hard to find the right people, and the hiring process can be arduous and Sisyphean. We have found a series of excellent teachers, but, like our members/friends, they rarely stay more than a year or two, succumbing to the deep forces of transience that mark our neighborhood and demographics.

Here is a typical job description we have posted:

Sunday School Teacher (ages 3-6)

Our arts-and-justice-oriented, LGBTQ-affirming, progressive faith community, First Church Somerville UCC, is in search of a Sunday School teacher.

3-6 year old "Godly Play" Montessori classroom: We will provide training for you to set up and run a Montessori-based, imaginative learning environment for our younger children. A lay volunteer from the church will assist you weekly. Experience with Godly Play welcomed, but not required. Ability to attend Godly Play training in the New England region helpful. See www.godlyplayfoundation.org for more information about Godly Play.

You are: a person of faith (any Christian denomination), loving, creative, progressive in your understanding of God and your orientation toward the Bible, responsible, enthusiastic, and at least 18 years old. We would prefer teachers who are available throughout the year and who are interested in longer-term commitments.

Hours and compensation: School hours are currently 8:45-10 a.m. and will be moving to 9:45-11 a.m. by April 2014. It's expected that you'll spend an hour each week preparing your lesson. Pay is $45/week, 34 weeks per year (there is no Sunday School one week per month).

Start date is flexible, but available now.

OUR CLASSROOMS

Currently our classrooms are divided like this:

0-3: Nursery

3-5: Godly Play I, Montessori-based biblical storytelling

5-7: Godly Play II (see above)

8-12: The Flying Hedgehogs (they chose their own classroom name years ago, and it stuck. They use the Sparkhouse curriculum these days, and most of them like it. We have also done workshop rotation and *Gather 'Round* but they didn't stick).

ALL AGES WORSHIP AND KIDS IN WORSHIP

One thing we feel strongly about at FCS is that our children are not the future, they are the Now.

We worship intergenerationally (ages 3 and up, with nursery open every Sunday of the year for ages 0-3) once a month so that:

- Kids learn that worship isn't "something for grownups."
- Adults learn that worship isn't "something for grownups."
- Families can worship together (whether they want to or not).
- Our Sunday school teachers get a Sabbath, when they can choose to worship with us or sleep in or attend worship elsewhere.

Our All Ages worship is not materially different from "regular" church, but we do some or all of the following things:

- Preacher story-tells the scripture rather than reads it, or has an older child read it.
- Child will be co-liturgist with a parent or adult friend (a big role: see "Liturgist Guidelines for Sunday Worship" in the Appendix).
- Preacher preaches from the floor, often without a manuscript, inviting all the children to sit in the first few pews.
- Preacher incorporates dialogical technique/sermon callbacks/ kinesthetic or multi-sensory learning into the sermon time, uses puppets or Godly Play technique or other ways of getting out of the manuscript box.
- There is no stand-alone choral anthem.
- Children's choir or family choir sings.
- Children collect offering (this happens *every* week at First Church, not just on All Ages Sundays).
- Children light Advent candles and participate in other hands-on liturgical practices.
- Songs are shorter, employ call-and-response.
- We print a kids' bulletin that has *only* song lyrics and some pictures for coloring.
- We stash a big basket at the back with sacred books, crayons and coloring books to keep little hands busy.
- Rocking chairs at the back wait for nursing mothers.
- Children have a role in baptism: swirling the water, shouting key phrases, etc.

On other Sundays, our kids don't start out in worship and leave after the scripture or children's message. This model didn't work for us for a number of reasons: we were a "late to church" church; so many of our kids/parents were new that they would have to accompany their kids out of worship to get them settled in the classroom, which was disruptive to their worship experience; and kids would miss the "best" part of worship: communion.

Instead, we have our kids start the hour in Sunday school and come in toward the end of the prayers of the people. They collect the offering and bring it up for blessing (sometimes with antics but with an overwhelming sense of reverence). They are present for the final hymn and the blessing. And if there is anything "extra" in worship: blessing of the backpacks, a baptism, communion or other special liturgies—they are there to fully participate.

ADULT FAITH FORMATION

If people choose to go to church in this day and age, it's not for lack of other social options. If all they want is friends and activities, Meetup can deliver that more specifically and efficiently than any church. Which is not to say that friendship/fellowship is not a tremendously important part of the way we engage whenever we come together as church! But it's not the first or most important part.

The first and most important part is spiritual formation. Spiritual formation is about our relationship with God, about learning what it might mean to be a follower of Jesus, about learning to deal with anxiety and worry/vocational questions/money/sex/relationships/parenting/etc. in a holy way. It is giving people the right shoes and gear to take their spiritual journey to a new level.

Some of the programs/ministries we have run for spiritual formation include:

Imponderables: a.k.a. The Imponderable Questions of Life. We'd gather once a month at a local bar for dinner/beer/soda, and discuss one Big Question in a theological vein: like War, or Abortion, being careful to have a moderator (a.k.a someone who had planned some talking points) and a behavioral covenant that observed mutual respect for all opinions and positions.

Rooftop People: A small peer-based theological reflection group based on the healing story in Mark 2, for doctors, therapists, ministers and other professional "healers," a chance to bring case studies, work through thorny issues in their practices and pray together for mutual support.

Lenten House Church: Every year, a different series. We've used Rob Bell's excellent Nooma videos, we have taken our denomination's Constitution to heart (especially the phrase "the responsibility of this church in every generation to make this faith its own") and written new creeds relevant to modern-day politics and culture; we have talked about the Seven Deadly Sins. We gather at a house (or at church) for simple candlelit worship, a simple vegan soup supper, a little bit of teaching and a little bit of small-group discussion.

Prayer Partners: For devotional seasons, like Advent or Lent, we will offer to set people up as prayer partners. The concept is simple: you and your prayer partner talk on the phone or in person (no texting! no email!) once a week for fifteen minutes. You talk confidentially about things that really matter, and tell what you'd like your prayer partner to pray for you that week. Then you actually pray together, if both of you are comfortable doing that, or you covenant to pray individually later for your partner.

Not all the prayer partnerships "take" equally, but many do—and they have the added benefit of broadening the pastoral care base of the church: people get more "ministers" within the priesthood of all believers.

Hot Buttons Bible Study: We've done Bible study series on radically relevant topics like sex, money, and a very well-attended one on fundamentalist Christian theology called Defense Against the Dark Arts.

All Church Retreat: We started our winter retreat small, and now about 70 people attend our annual all-church retreat, including marrieds and singles, parents and those without kids. This past year we made it a two-night retreat, with lots of Sabbath time, a little bit of teaching/learning something spiritual that is applicable to daily living, lots of singing songs around the fireplace, card games and board games and wine and cocoa, snow-labyrinth walking and sledding.

Other Retreats: As our congregation has grown, we offer more niche retreats: Family Retreat, Women's Retreat, Wilderness Retreat. We try to keep the barrier to entry low: low-cost, late-RSVP-OK, local. We capitalize on in-house resources: a woman who had just bought her first house and loves to entertain held our first women's retreat at her home. My farmer friends offered their backyard in the boonies for our family retreat. We cook all our own meals. Something about being together, overnight, with bedhead in the morning, snoring, washing up together after meals, taking turns doing chores, makes people vulnerable and connected to each other (not to mention to God) in important ways. Wilderness Retreat is a three-day, two-night wilderness adventure. It's open to anyone who loves the outdoors and is comfortable carrying a pack up and down mountains. We camp in the backcountry with no bathrooms or showers or beds and seek to meet God in the beauty, power, and simplicity of the natural world.

Mission Trips: Mission trips are an incredible way to build group loyalty and connection, and disciple people in the Way of Jesus. The arduousness (and sometimes peril) of travel first puts stress on, then strengthens, our bonds. The work we do, whether it's with Habitat building houses one state away or across the world in an impoverished nation, reminds us of Matthew 25's urging to serve the least of these in order to serve Jesus.

Often, those who go on mission trips emerge as stable, committed leaders when they return. At our church, we take a biennial intergenerational trip to the Casa San Jose orphanage in Colima, Mexico. After our third trip there, the group that came back was so energized that they founded a nonprofit that raises tens of thousands of dollars annually for the orphanage (and that particular trip spawned several weddings, a nice side-benefit).

PRAYER TEAM AND PRAYERS OF THE PEOPLE

One of the most important ways we have deepened our individual and collective spiritual life is in our prayers of the people. When we pray, we *really* pray. See the "Worship" section for more info on how our prayers in worship evolved. We also have a Prayer Team. It is small: people join only if they can pledge to really pray the prayers of our community every week. We have a "prayer card" insert in our bulletin weekly, and we post the prayers, in the hand of the person who has written them, on Dropbox on Sunday afternoon for the prayer team members to read. We also have a Yahoo! group listserv on which we can disseminate prayers that come up throughout the week.

We talk a lot about prayer in our life together, in office hours conversations, in sermons and other venues: people for the most part—when they come to us and before they get very involved as leaders—feel ill-equipped to pray, feel like they don't really know how to pray or that their prayers are "not good enough" (unless they are among our addicts in recovery: then they are pros!).

I talk about Simone Weil's definition of prayer, "absolutely unmixed attention," Teresa of Avila's "simple talking with God as a cherished friend," and Anne Lamott's "Help Thanks Wow" modes of prayer, to lower the bar. I encourage people to pray every day, and to pray as they can, not as they can't (e.g. don't try to start with an hour of centering prayer a day if they are naturally kinetic people! Try walking prayer for five minutes instead). It's spiritual practice, not spiritual perfect, I remind them.

We pray all the time when we are together, at office hours, at church meetings, at pastoral counseling sessions, and I am not above putting people on the spot to close or open us in prayer, so they know it's not just something the paid professionals can do.

NEW MEMBERS' ORIENTATION

We hold three new members' classes during each cycle. In the first class, the bar is very low: it's a ten-dollar tour of the church, including closets and messy places, usually when Big Meeting Brunch committees are meeting so people can see the work of the church, and overhear some of it (we also might ask a rep from each committee to say hi and spend 30 seconds talking about their work as they move through). As we move through the church, we might tell a little history, or sing a hymn, or talk about our vision for what's next for the ministry in that particular space, to enlist them in the vision.

The second meeting is hosted at a home. It is a chance to learn a bit more about our denomination, the United Church of Christ, and to talk through the Membership Promises they will make if they choose to join. We talk about our theology of baptism, doubting and believing, our theology of communion and how it connects to the member practices of giving, attendance and leadership in the community. There are still some looky-loos at this point in the process, and I make it clear what the expectations of formal membership are (primarily: pledged giving to the church, regular attendance and taking on some kind of leadership role) so that people know what they are getting into if they choose to take the membership step at this time.

The third meeting is for people who have committed to joining. We have crepes and champagne/sparkling cider at the church parsonage with me and my family on the Friday evening before the formal joining ceremony on Sunday. We celebrate their joining, have them fill out spiritual gifts inventories, and we all take turns telling our faith stories.

The faith-story-sharing is just about the high point of my job. You would not believe the stuff that comes out at that sharing of stories. Lots of tears, lots of laughter, lots of gifted and moving God-talk from people who by and large "don't know how to pray" and "have a lot of doubts."

And, on Sunday, they join. A sample of our new members' joining liturgy is in the Appendix. We always take nuggets out of the faith stories (being careful not to betray confidences), so that the congregation can quick-meet these people who are making promises to them. We give them homemade boutonnieres to distinguish new members on their joining Sunday. My friend's church has a luncheon to honor new members. Someday we'll be on the stick enough to do that!

We have, in the past, had the previous new members' class provide hospitality for the new new members' class. This has the happy function of creating a reunion for the previous class, as well as linking up newish people who aren't yet saturated with relationships; and it reminds them all that "the one who would be first must be last and servant of all," that when we become members of a church, we are, in the words of Mike Piazza, a church growth great, "taking off a bib, and putting on an apron."

ACTUALLY, YOU KNOW WHAT? DON'T WORRY ABOUT JOINERS

All that said, don't worry about formal membership. Some denominational executives are still all about membership numbers. We filled out an application for a big mortgage this past year, to pay for the part of the renovation to our building that our capital campaign couldn't quite cover. We had a great story, and great numbers, *but* the number that was not so great was our formal membership: it hadn't budged in 10 years, apparently stalled out at about 140.

I explained to the mortgage lender (who, blessedly, is a church person) that people came to our church, and loved their church, and gave to their church, and some of them joined—but not all of them, not even most. *Generalization alert*: It's a mark of the Gen X, Gen Y and Millenials that they are not big joiners. They don't trust institutions, they like to keep things loose, they are not big RSVPers. *But* when they find something they love they will keep coming and support it in the ways that matter.

So maybe don't worry about membership so much. Run good and meaningful membership classes for those new people who *do* want to join—a welcome into the heart of things, is what I call it. But don't live and die by that number. There are so many other important numbers to measure when calculating vitality. You can see how we measure health on the "By the Numbers" we run on the back of the pledge card every fall.

And a coda: *do* clean your membership rolls, early and often. There will be feelings about this! But it's important to do for the congregation to keep a realistic and healthy baseline of where they actually are. Depending on how your governance works, you don't have to alert the inactive member about their new status (which can feel shaming, or hurt the relationship)—you can just put them into a different category ("inactive" versus severed). We use two criteria to determine whether someone qualifies as an active member, and they only need to satisfy one: they are still pledging formally, or they have attended worship once in the last year. Local shut-ins are the only exemption. Be ruthless!

CHAPTER THREE

Pastoral Care

• • •

I'll talk about office hours in a bit, which is the primary vehicle by which our church's ministers offer pastoral care. I also invite people, if they can't make it to office hours, to make an appointment with me. More and more, I don't meet with them in my office, but I'll offer to go for a walk and a talk. I find that talking in parallel (versus face to face) and while moving often helps people open up more. Plus we both get exercise and vitamin D. Plus then we're not locked into the hour-long meeting format that an office seems to warrant, no matter the size or complexity (or simplicity) of the issue.

EMAIL AND FACEBOOK AS PASTORAL CARE VENUES

My congregation is very plugged-in. They far prefer email or texting to phone calls or in-person meetings. I check in with people a lot by email, and every single time I write an email to a leader about a church work issue, I always preface it by first asking them how they are and referencing what they might be going through in their daily life: to acknowledge the whole person and not just their work for their church.

You'll read more about our liturgist program in the "Worship" section, but working with our Sunday morning liturgist each week on the drafts of their liturgy is really pastoral theology at its most rewarding: helping wounded healers work out their theology of grace and redemption about a formerly (and perhaps still) painful problem or issue.

I go back and forth on whether or not I really like Facebook, but it has been undeniably helpful as an outreach tool and, surprisingly, as a mode of offering pastoral care. Many, many things come up on Facebook—vocational issues or changes, death of a pet, family losses, etc.—that parishioners would not "trouble" me with by mentioning it to me directly. I can then follow up online with Facebook comments or private message, or by email or in person, depending on the nature of the issue and how much of a response it may warrant.

A little later I'll talk about using Google Voice as a way of giving people the means to contact the pastor(s) in case of pastoral emergency, which makes it easy to have the call forward to a different pastor or a lay leader when the solo pastor is on vacation.

SMALL GROUPS FOR ALL

Every summer, we suspend regular committee meetings in July, and assign everyone who currently attends worship to a small group. These groups are loosely based on affinities (like people with small kids, or active people, or geographical location), but we also leave a good degree of it up to the Holy Spirit.

We tell people: you don't have to go, but you have a group if you want one—and you are wanted. Each group ideally has two strong co-leaders, people gifted at group dynamics and building community. The group is free to determine where and when they will meet (weekly for four to six weeks), and what they will do.

The pastors provide talking points or "curricula" for the leaders if they want them, but most prefer to do their own thing—with the one guideline that they check in with each other at the beginning and do a deepish group prayer at the end of their time together.

Some groups are wildly successful and people really bond; others are less successful. It's really about the luck of the draw and the giftedness of the leaders. But we feel it's important to provide newcomers a lot of easy entry points into community, and this is just one more.

CARING FOR PEOPLE THROUGH LIFE EVENTS

This is something we do pretty well, but need to learn how to do better as we grow, honestly. Along with our two settled pastors, our ten deacons have traditionally handled caring for people through life events (illness, childbirth and adoption, divorce, death). Deacons are laypeople, among the most spiritually mature in the congregation, though with no formal training, who are commissioned to serve three-year terms. They organize people to cook for new parents, are great at showing up for wakes and funerals and putting on receptions after funerals for our elders who don't have family to do that for them. For the occasional high-visibility church member who needs rides or other more consistent support, they have been able to provide it.

We also have several wonderful retired clergy or extra-parochial clergy (chaplains, interim ministers, and clergy who serve in settings other than parishes) in our congregation who will visit folks in the hospital if the settled pastor is away, and offer other kinds of pastoral care. A couple of years ago we had a "Compassionate Caregivers" small group, people who were trained in active listening, confidentiality, praying, boundary setting, etc., who would visit our homebound elders or others in need.

In spite of these gifted people, I have wished, over the years, that we had the capacity and know-how to run a wider lay visitation ministry such as Called to Care or Stephen Ministry. Since most of our folks are working outside the home full time (or more than full time! We have no stay at home moms or dads in the congregation, and very few retired folks) or in school full time, it just doesn't seem viable. But I'm open!

CHAPTER FOUR

Pastoral Self-Care and Administration

● ● ●

THE PAINSTAKING ADMINISTRATIVENESS OF GROWING A CHURCH

Doubtless there are magic leaders in magic, radically-open-to-the-Gospel cultures who can grow churches quickly. Myself, I've always been jealous of Rob Bell and his Mars Hill church experiment in an abandoned mall in Michigan.

But I don't know how to build a church quickly, or if it's even possible in my (Christian-resistant, even hostile) neck of the woods. I'm heartened/disheartened by some evidence that even megachurches have high churn, the suggestion that the average tenure of engagement is about 18 months before people fall away. I'm heartened because it maybe means their methods are more about hype and entertainment than actual engagement—the consumer model of religion. And I'm disheartened because: if those big churches with their deep resources can't make it work, what hope is there for the rest of us?

What I know how to do is build churches one person and relationship at a time. It's too soon to tell—maybe ask me at the Rapture, when we're waiting in line for our holy elevator to Heaven—but I think our growth is reliable, and will endure.

This kind of growth is less about flash—radical outreach and dramatic worship—than it is about helping people assimilate into the Body of Christ, one and two and five at a time. We are high-touch pastors in our church: this doesn't mean, at our size (the low-middle end of "program size" church) that everyone expects to have a personal relationship with us. But we are engaged with every single person who sticks, we keep a detailed spreadsheet on sticky people, and do a lot of traffic direction: remembering details, connecting folks for different purposes at different times.

Like what I was just doing: remembering that the new lesbian couple who are both seminary grads live in the neighborhood that is just starting a neighborhood potluck at the home of a blind couple who are a little nervous about hosting, chasing everyone's digits down and getting them connected. It means holding a lot of data in your head—as well as in Google docs.

The open secret is that vital ministry is 10% inspiration, 90% administration. It's not sexy, but it's holy.

SELF-CARE PACKAGE

A lot of ink has been spilled about self-care in seminaries and clergy groups over the last couple of decades. Since the term "workaholic" was actually coined by a Baptist minister to describe his colleagues back in the early 20th century, maybe the rise of Self-Care as a concept was a necessary counter-movement.

But it seems to me that the term "self-care" has become a front in some instances for being a little lazy, or letting oneself off the hook from doing work that is just really hard, no bones about it.

A colleague of mine said that maybe we should talk less about self-care and more about self-differentiation. Rabbi Edwin Friedman said that self-differentiation was "the willingness to take responsibility for your own emotional well-being and destiny." Doesn't that soar?

Another way of saying this is: self-differentiation is owning what you believe, what you need, and what you like to do—and also knowing where you end and your (sweetheart, child, parent, job, church, nemesis, fill-in-the-blank) begins.

It took me a long time to get the hang of self-differentiation, with a lot of workaholism along the way, and false starts toward real Sabbath—Sabbath, a commandment, which God intends for every one of Her children and what pastors have to model better than anybody if our people are going to feel free to practice it as well.

The commitment to rest and play did not become wholly central to my life until I got, and survived, cancer—and I had lots of other forces urging me to Sabbath already: young kids! And a husband I liked to spend time with! And and and. Even now, after cancer, I still need to make course corrections all the time.

We all have to learn self-care/differentiation in our own way, in our own time. Here's some of what I do to practice good self-differentiation, to stay calm and happy for the long haul of this vocation:

1. Spiritual direction: at least once a month. I choose my spiritual directors carefully—they have to be good, really good, and wiser than I believe myself to be, or I won't listen to them. When I find a good one, I stick with them for a long time.
2. Remember the Sabbath and keep it wholly. In my early days of ministry, when I was less comfortable being my real self with the people I served, I actually started leaving town on my day off. I'd go grocery shopping, or see a movie, a couple towns away just so I would be less likely to bump into parishioners and suddenly have to switch the Rev. "on."
3. Do things you love to do, things that have nothing to do with ministry! Read novels, or trashy magazines; go bike riding for fun, not to commute; watch Youtube videos that make you laugh because they are so inappropriate, not because they are sermon fodder.

4. Exercise. It's a dreadful word, and an awesome experience: to claim your body back for yourself and for the One who made you, to steal your flesh back from Mammon and a host of other greedy ego-driven gods who would consume all of us and give nothing back if given the chance.
5. Cook and eat really good homemade food! I know all about the fat wars, and I'm not going to get into it here, but: one of the biggest factors that correlates with being overweight is eating at home vs. eating out. Duh! Who would go to the trouble to make, say, duck fat french fries in their own kitchen? But I would totally rock that in a restaurant—the sharing size, all by myself. I mean, I'm not going to *pay* someone to make me steamed kale, when I can do that myself at home! That said, kale is a more reliable bet for the kind of energy and health I want long-term.
6. If you're in a good relationship, have lots of *excellent sex*. Nothing makes me feel like my life is *mine* (and God's, and my spouse's) than getting jiggy with regularity.
7. Take vacation. *Really.* And be truly away. Even if it takes you a day or two to unplug at the beginning of it, give your congregation (or your pastoral colleague) the satisfaction and confidence of knowing they can handle it on their own—that it really *doesn't* all depend on you. Nobody loves a martyr, or an egomaniac. And you know what? Nobody loves a workaholic either. They just make things harder for the rest of us.
8. When all else fails, remember that it's not your church; it's not even your people's church. *This church belongs to Jesus*. And while Jesus wants you to do your part, you do not have ultimate responsibility for it. Now go home!

WORKING HARD

That said, this church renewal business is hard work, and there's a lot of it. Not everybody is cut out for it. There is just too much inertia to overcome here at the end of the Christian empire, too many fights along the way, too much risk, too much plank-walking, and a durn steep learning curve.

If you are a hardcore introvert, or even a mild introvert, doing renewal in a truly dying church is probably not for you. Likewise if you have chronic health issues, it will be very difficult to give both your body and your church the attention each deserves to function optimally. If you have a family that loves to see you: well. It really helps if they like your church and want to be there.

Our church first hired me as a three-quarter time pastor, with a three-quarter time salary and a full-time giant parsonage including basic utilities. The parsonage was next door, which I know has been a perilous experience for some of you, but it really helped us, for a long time. Cutting my commute time to zero meant more time with family and more time for church.

As our church grew, they kept offering me full-time hours, and I kept refusing. Even though I worked, more or less, 40-50 hours a week, I personally appreciated the expectation that only 30 hours a week was *required* of me.

I also encouraged them to take the money they would have paid me and spend it on other staff, so I could begin to outsource, to other talented people, the work of ministry. Having a paid administrator, paid nursery caregiver, and paid Sunday school teachers all helps our church serve people ably and well.

Five years after I came to First Church, we had grown enough that we could think about hiring an associate pastor. We secured grant funding from several different sources to fund a half-time position for two years—we called this our Minister of Outreach. More on this in the section on Staffing. Our first Associate Pastor ended up staying for two and a half years. She left to take another church, by pure coincidence, on the same day I announced to the congregation my cancer diagnosis.

We hired a single full-time "Support Pastor" for the year that I was in cancer treatment. He did a great job. The church didn't grow much, but it didn't shrink much, either—which is what we might have expected during such a crisis. I continued to live next door, but I did very little: I mentored the support pastor, meeting weekly; I went to worship and sat in the back pew. I served on the new associate pastor search committee, because the senior/associate relationship is paramount in the life and health of a church.

After I survived cancer, I wanted to make some changes in my life and priorities, and sought to renegotiate my contract. I realized, no matter how long my life turned out to be, time was short. Even though my oncologist was fairly confident my cancer would not come back, I knew that however long the rest of my life turned out to be, I did not want to work it away. I wasn't ready to quit and read (or write) novels, but I had to build in better efficiencies, and bracket my hours.

I told our church moderator that instead of getting paid for three-quarter time and working full time, I would like to get paid half time and really work three-quarter time—and hire a three-quarter time associate instead of a half time associate. I know, boundary alert! I love my church and I was also in a financial position to do this, having a spouse who works full time.

Thank goodness, our then-moderator is a preacher's kid, who knows how to advocate for clergy. He said, "How about if we pay you three-quarter time and you work three-quarter time? And we hire a three-quarter time associate pastor to support the work of the church?"

That's exactly what we did—and though it was a bit of a crunch the first year, it totally paid for itself. We hired the right person, and worship attendance jumped 40% the year after he came. We'd been growing steadily all those years, but something about the magic of the ninth year of my tenure and *this* staff—we made a great leap forward.

It wasn't easy learning how to work the hours I was paid for instead of always working a little bit more. It sure helps to have something outside of church that gives you soul-satisfaction, which is a much better thing than the ego-satisfaction being a workaholic pastor provides. Ego is a hungry beast, never satisfied, always looking for the next rush.

That said, I'm not sure that we would have turned the corner if I'd really only worked 30 hours a week all those years.

I am still three-quarter time, and now I use the extra quarter to be home with my kids after school, to work on writing projects not directly related to the parish, to say yes to new experiences and opportunities. I work smarter, not harder, with those 30 hours, and so far, it seems to be working out.

Here is what else helps in figuring out how to work smarter, not harder: interrogate everything you do. Ask each thing you do: Is this task really *necessary?* Are you doing it because you (or the church) have always done it that way? Is there a better way to do it? Does this task line up with your stated vision and strategy for meeting that vision?

Ask yourself: Who and what are the demographics and people I should really be serving? Am I spending my time proportionally, or am I spending more time, say, with cranky unhealthy people than with healthy people who really want to grow spiritually? Am I spending too much time with longtime members who already have roots and relationships, and not enough with newcomers—or better yet, with people who haven't yet set foot through the door?

Of course, all of these shifts are very threatening to both the cranky people and the long-timers. It takes time to get even the healthy long-timers, who are your main allies, on board with the idea that you should be spending most of your time with newcomers. It takes a big culture shift—start right away! Confront them with their own words: say, if you want to grow, really if you do, this is what it means.

Two of the big efficiencies I have built into my schedule: weekly Office Hours, and Big Meeting Brunch.

WEEKLY OFFICE HOURS

I discovered I was wasting a lot of time setting up individual meetings with parishioners. I was also seeing a disproportionate number of people who were chronically stuck: It is a sad truism of ministry that the people who most need your help are also the ones least likely to benefit from it.

In the meantime, there were plenty of healthy people in my parish who had hard things going on, and I would only find out after the fact. I'd say "Why didn't you tell me! We could have met to talk and pray about that." Every single one of them answered, "I didn't want to bother you, I know how busy you are, and you have people with much bigger problems."

First of all: pastors should never seem so busy as to be unapproachable. We have failed if we are doing this!

Second of all: I'll say it again. We should be spending the vast majority of our time with healthy people and with new people. They are the ones who will really benefit from our wisdom and attention. And ministering to them will help them minister to others—it's a God-approved Ponzi scheme.

I stole a very simple and even retro idea from a friend of mine: I hold weekly office hours. I do it at a local café, 8:30-10 a.m., every Wednesday. I chose the Diesel Café, a wicked hipster, super-busy hub, because people go there, it's easy to get to and it's a quiet form of evangelism to folks who would not normally find themselves in contact with progressive Christians.

I have thought about putting up a table tent, "The Rev. Is In," but prefer, for now, to fly under the radar most days—though I did, for Ash Wednesday, wear a Roman collar and put up a sign on the wall that said

"Ashes to Go," which several strangers gladly availed themselves of, even in our religion-phobic city.

I try to make office hours inviolate and undeviating, unless I am on vacation. If I am inconsistent, people will lose track of when I am there and not come.

Anyone can come, and talk to me about anything. I get a booth, and people drop in and drop out. Sometimes people want one-on-one time—when people first walk up, I ask them if they need it—and if someone does, the gang holds the booth while I check into a "private" table for 10-30 minutes. The gang left behind at the table has a chance to bond, often established folks welcoming newbies, or even better: newbies with newbies, since neither one of them is yet saturated with relationships!

More and more, when I ask, "Do you need one-on-one time?" folks will hesitate, then say, "I guess I can share this with everybody." And then what happens is truly Holy Spirit work: they benefit not just from my wisdom and support, but also from the shared wisdom and support of everyone present. Deep connections are made. Life-altering advice exchanged. And then we hold hands and pray together, out loud and in front of all those hipsters and baristas.

Over the years, office hours has developed a crowd of regulars: unemployed folks who need some structure to get them out of bed, showered and ready for the day; new parents at home on maternity/paternity leave; students. I've held evening office hours, too, for people who work traditional hours, but they were much more inconsistently attended. I suspect this is because my heart wasn't really in it: I was out too much at night already, I really didn't want to be out and away from my family any more. You'll do what works for you and your people.

The best thing about office hours is the bang for the buck: the number of people I am able to see and connect with (on a given week, anywhere from 3-15!), and the number of healthy people who previously wouldn't have wanted to "bother me" but who benefit from a few minutes of the pastor's time to talk over a distressing matter. And, truth be told, I think I benefit more than anyone. It is one of the highlights of my week.

BIG MEETING BRUNCH

So, we are not one of those amazing renewal churches that has figured out how not to have committees. A clergy colleague of mine runs her entire church with six lay leaders! I am flabbergasted by this.

But it goes without saying that the archaic, committee-heavy structure of 50s-era churches doesn't work anymore. For one, the age of civil religion, when everybody went to church because everybody else went to church, and smart, willing stay-at-home moms were all casting about for something meaningful to do with their time were a dime a dozen—that day is done. You don't need 20 committees and 140 elected leaders to run a church with 30 people in worship.

What we have done at First Church, as far as governance, is ignore the committees that are obsolete (like Memorials and Bequests. That day, for the most part, is also done!), and create new *ad hoc* teams as needed: Outreach, Hospitality, Communications. We changed the name of some of them to reflect new foci, e.g. from Missions to Missions and Justice, to reflect that we didn't just want to write checks, we wanted active, sweaty engagement and relationships with the agencies we wrote checks *to.*

What I discovered, as the teams proliferated, was that I had more and more meetings to go to. I was out three, four, five nights a week. And not only was I getting worn out and mildly resentful, but the team members, many of whom were on multiple committees, were too. And the chairs were not all taking full ownership of their work and vision, but still turning too much to the pastors.

So, we came up with this solution. Truthfully, I came up with this solution and some of them kicked and screamed or passive-aggressively ignored it for quite a while, but it's been a few years now and it's working, quite well. We call it Big Meeting Brunch.

Our church is very electronic—we don't print much, we don't snail-mail much. We are able to get a lot done by email, using Google docs. So, because we can move things forward in between meetings by email, many of our committees get away with meeting only every two months. (For more, see the section on Electronica.)

But when they do meet, our committees and teams meet all at the same time, after worship, on the third Sunday of the month. This is Big Meeting Brunch. Big Meeting Brunch is split into two squads that toggle back and forth. The Alpha Squad is Hospitality, Outreach, Buildings and Grounds. The Omega Squad is Personnel, Communications, Mission & Justice.

Some teams meet every month, at a separate evening or early morning meeting, because the pace demands it: Church Council, Deacons, Finance, Children's Ministry. You can see why I got tired of going to meetings!

On Big Meeting Brunch Sundays after worship, we spend a few minutes connecting with friends or newbies at coffee hour, then head off to our various teams. Often, the Moderator or Hospitality Team will make up trays of bagels, Danish, fruit that teams can take with them as fuel. Teams meet as long as they need to, but usually are done within 60 to 75 minutes.

They use this time to build community and check in with each other (an easy way to do this is to ask everyone to name their High and Low for the previous week), to move through their agenda, and to take at least 5 minutes to pray together at the end of the meeting, for each other's and the world's needs. Then they get to move into the rest of their Sabbath!

n.b: A church meeting, like the planning of a wedding, will fill whatever time you allot. You should never, never say at the beginning of a church meeting, "We have a light agenda tonight! We should be able to be out of here early," because that meeting will run till Judgment Day. It's the Murphy's Law of church meetings.

Important: we also keep the Nursery open with paid nursery care during Big Meeting Brunch meetings. It helps young parents say yes to leadership in the church, without whom there would be a big gap.

Big Meeting Brunch solves several problems at once:

- It allows parents with young kids to be involved in leadership, without burdening spouses with child care and creating resentment toward the church.
- It allows pastors to guide discussions and committee work rather than be the *de facto* chair of every committee. I communicate with committee chairs a week or two before Big Meeting Brunch, either by email or in person, about what will be on the agenda. Then, I circulate to as many committee meetings as I can get to, trying not to privilege one over another.
- It allows laypeople to truly take ownership of their church and its vision, without their pastors micromanaging them.
- It invites newbies into the work and play of the church with a very low barrier to entry—all of our BMB meetings are open to the public, and they can drop in or out as it pleases them.
- It means that laypeople can only serve on one of those teams at a time (or, technically, two, since the squads toggle back and forth), which puts healthy artificial boundaries around their volunteering so they don't burn out (and also prevents power-grabbing to a degree!).
- It means team members get to see each other's work—so no one team gets into the idolatrous mindset that their work is more important, or the false notion they work harder than any other team, which is toxic to the Body of Christ.
- It means *zero* time is wasted on endless email threads trying to find a good time to meet, which is deeply enervating so that there's no energy left when the team finally does sit down.

- It frees up evenings for *ad hoc* projects in the church, midweek creative worship, or having dinner with friends or family and going to bed on time! Yahoo!

Last word on Big Meeting Brunch: most new shifts in our church take six weeks to six months to seed. This one took more like three years. Maybe some of it was my fault, because I didn't introduce it in the right way, or it wasn't consistent enough in application, or I didn't do enough reminding ahead of time that BMB was coming up. Teams would "go rogue" and forget they were supposed to meet, then spend a month trying to find a good time to meet, then discover that half their team members weren't there anyhow.

I just kept saying, please, let's try this. Your pastor's mental health and the health of her family—and, I think, your health and longevity as a vital member of this your church—depend upon it. They finally got the picture. It's not perfect, but it works, more or less.

[*excursus*: I think all the ink wasted on Committee structure versus Ministry-based approach is heavy on jargon and light on content. I think "Committee" is a loaded word and immediately sets folks to yawning or running for the hills, and "Ministry" or "Team" invokes holy vocation and shared power, which is good—but they're all just different words for the same thing, which is the work and play of the Church.]

JOB DESCRIPTION

The third and final thing that really helped improve my work efficiency was having a clear job description and profile. Our previous associate pastor and I didn't have clear roles, and because of that, there was a lot of redundancy in how we spent our time. Both of us would visit every sick person. Both of us would be at every single meeting. I think, at the time, we thought it made individuals and committees/teams feel "good" to have support from both of us—but functionally it was also about making ourselves feel OK and "good enough" as pastors.

Our current associate pastor and I know exactly who is supposed to be doing what. I know I can count on him to get his stuff done, and he can count on me to get my stuff done. Because we're really clear about this, we both feel comfortable helping the other person out if they are sick, or swamped. Because we're really clear about this, it eliminates a lot of the jockeying for position and ego-trampling that is too often the hallmark of the Senior Pastor/Associate Pastor relationship. I also know that when he is doing well, it makes me look good! So it's in my interest to support him and help him develop his gifts to the fullest.

See my job profile in the Appendix. We developed it after that fateful conversation with our then-moderator. He demanded that I show him how I would limit my hours so the church could learn how to have healthy expectations for what three-quarter time meant, and model to other churches how to care for its pastors.

ELIMINATING REDUNDANCY: HELPS AND HINTS FOR TIME MANAGEMENT

For a time, after we got a second pastor, the folks in the church thought we would both visit every sick person, both follow up on every pastoral care issue, both attend every meeting—but that was not a good use of our time, and it didn't ultimately further the vision of the church; it just reinforced a sense that pastors were somehow more "important" than lay folks and that neither one of us was "enough" on our own.

If you aren't lucky enough to have a clergy colleague, well, you won't have a partner to lean on, but you don't have to worry about redundancy! But it is worth thinking about what lay folks can take off the pastor's plate, as you shift the focus of your ministry hours to reflect the congregation's commitment to being a growing/renewing church.

Following is a short list of things my pastoral colleague and I did to eliminate redundancy in our job profiles, make sure the work was split equitably, and foster a sense of competency in our "priesthood of all believers" congregation.

Google voice for pastoral emergencies: Google has a cool program where you can assign a telephone number that forwards to any phone line you choose. My colleague and I trade off weeks being "on-call," so that people only have to call one number in case of pastoral emergency. If you don't answer the call, the caller can leave a voicemail, which you can access by email (Google will even email you a transcript!). This is a *free* service.

Visiting shut-ins and those in hospital: When a parishioner goes into the hospital, whoever first makes contact with them says "I will discuss this with Jeff/Molly and one of us will come and see you soon, if that is something you would appreciate." There are also excellent training programs to teach layfolks the skills they need to offer a mature ministry of presence to sick or very elderly/disabled folks: Called To Care and Stephen Ministries come to mind. We developed our own in-house training, called Compassionate Caregivers, which taught our layfolks about active listening, boundary awareness, and how to pray aloud with others, among other things. We sent them out in pairs, just like Jesus.

Email: Honestly, I am not very good at bracketing how much time I spend on email. Some tricks: work in a place without wifi. Stop answering emails after a specific time each day (noon, 3 p.m.—or, if you start at 5 a.m. like me, 9 a.m.!). Delay replying to emails for a half-day, a day, or more, to shift expectations around how quickly you will answer email. The faster you answer email, the more emails people will generate. It's OK to let some things marinate. The more time you spend on email, the less time you have for: 1) sitting in cafes or taking walks with parishioners, 2) going to community events where you will make new relationships and establish the church as a presence, 3) family and self.

One thing I *do not* do anymore is engage unhappy parishioners by email, or respond to them if they write to me. You know what

I'm talking about: the email subject line says "A concern," and you have to scroll down five times to read the entire length of the email. You get mad, then you get sad, then you spend two hours crafting your carefully written response. Then they send *their* carefully written response. And it keeps going around.

My colleague reminds me that most of these folks have a lot of time to craft carefully written responses. You don't. The time you spend on this activity will not, I repeat *not*, get your (or your adversary) the ends you desire. Nobody ever read an adversary's carefully crafted email and had a Eureka! moment, falling all over themselves in an effort to make amends for their bad or misguided behavior. The only tried and true way to resolve conflict is to sit down face to face.

I tell folks that I will meet with them in person, and that I will meet on their turf if that helps them feel stronger. If they say they are more articulate in writing, I say great, write out your concern and read it to me, while we sit together. If it would help to have a third person present, so you feel supported, I say, bring them along.

Christianity is an incarnational religion and we should meet in the flesh—it is only in this way that we can communicate nuance, body language, and have a real dialogue.

Shopping: I never knew there would be so much shopping in parish ministry! Really, it's a whole extra aspect of the job. One I rather like, if I admit it to myself. *But* there are some shopping sprees better left to others, so you have time to do pastoral care or make your sermon darn good instead of just good enough.

Find out who in your church loves to shop. Be clear with them what the budget is, and the materials you have in mind for the Advent craft workshop/Maundy Thursday Last Supper Feast, then set them free and release expectations beyond that.

Or if you are going to do the shopping yourself, use the Internet, and plan ahead so you don't have to waste church money paying for expedited shipping.

Also, find out who the obsessive tidiers in your congregation are, and empower them to come up with good storage systems so you're not re-buying supplies you already have.

Soft Hours: There are a lot of "soft hours" in ministry—meals at the homes of parishioners, thinking about sermons while driving or exercising, the aforementioned shopping. I count some of these hours as a sort of tithe on top of what I work already, and some of them as my 30 hours. Anything I am doing, that I wouldn't be doing if I weren't the pastor of our church, I count as work. Even if it's fun, it's work.

Clergy Groups: Going to every denominational gathering, town-based interfaith or ecumenical meeting or clergy coffee klatch could be a full time job in and of itself. And face it: sometimes what happens at these gatherings is complaining about how badly things are going at our churches or gloating about how well things are going at our churches, or both at the same time, which is really boggling. You go needing collaboration and collegiality, and leave feeling worse than when you came.

Choose carefully those meetings that will really yield something for you, for God, and for Christ's church. Don't just meet for the sake of meeting, because it makes you feel official.

MINISTERIAL CARE COMMITTEE

At the first church I served, Pastor Parish Relations committees were just coming into vogue, and we started one for both pastors. It worked well enough—until there was conflict in the church, and then the good folks on our committee thought their role was to "mediate" between us and the cranky people.

When I came to Somerville, my terribly wonderful people decided:

they didn't want a pastor parish relations committee. They wanted to provide me (and, now, our associate pastor) with a group that would be unrepentantly in support of their pastor, and they named it the Ministerial Care Committee. We meet every 4-6 weeks. They were some of the first people I told about my miscarriages, my cancer diagnosis. They were the people who took my kids to Chuck E. Cheese and made casseroles when my mom died. They are among the most mature people in the congregation—the people who understand family systems and conflict, who can hold confidences, who understand they are *not* my friends and *not* in my inner circle, but people charged with making sure I exercise good self-care strategies.

They give me courage when I have hard work to do. They challenge me in important ways—they are not "yes men" and women, but people who are very clear-eyed about the ways in which our church needs to grow.

They are not an anonymous complaint box for other members of the church to use. They are charged with "listening" for anxiety or fault lines in our congregation and having a supportive conversation with me about how we can lower anxiety or understand and communicate the vision better to the wider church. Every time we meet, we talk about me, and the church—not their own problems or their peeves. When we part, each of the three of them, in turn, prays for me, and I keep silent. These people are a great gift to me and a reason why I will be able to have a long tenure at my current church, even through the inevitable very hard times!

STAFF

Because I've read a gazillion books/blogs/articles about a new church plant's explosive growth, and always thought, "How the hell did they do any of that—really, logistically—like the hiring and training and supporting and retention of staff alone is a killer!," I thought I would tell you how and when we hired everybody on our staff. Note: this is based on my faulty memory! I would not swear to this time frame in a court of law.

2003: Hired solo pastor (me!). Other staff: 10 hour/week music director/accompanist and 10 hour/week custodian/sexton.

2004: Hired 6 hour/week church administrator.

2005: Administrator raised to 10 hours/week. Hired student minister 15 hours/week. Split music position into Music Director and Accompanist.

2006: Administrator raised/15 hours/week (partially grant-funded).

2007: Hired Sunday school teacher for one-room schoolhouse (3 hours/week). Hired half-time associate pastor (fully grant-funded).

2008: Hired nursery coordinator.

2009: Hired second Sunday school teacher. Administrator raised to half-time.

2010: Transitioned from one three-quarter-time and one half-time pastor to one full-time support pastor, for one year, during cancer.

2011: Transitioned to two three-quarter-time pastors.

2012: Hired third Sunday school teacher.

2013: Hired assistant music director (3-6 hours/week). Increased associate pastor hours to 35 hours/week.

2014: New hire: Director of Family Ministry, to oversee growing Sunday school.

Our entire staff: lead pastor (34 hours/week), associate pastor (38 hours/week), church administrator (20 hours/week), director of family ministry (10 hours/week), music director (6-12 hours/week), assistant music director (3-6 hours/week), custodian (15 hours/week), nursery (2 hours/week), 3 Sunday school teachers (3 hours/week including prep), and sometimes a student minister.

We will continue to raise pastor hours until both pastors are full time. Onward and upward!

So many other people have written so wisely about multi-staff church settings that I am not going to say much here, but I want to flag a couple things. The most important things about growing our staff have been: doing a rigorous search process so we find the best possible candidate, setting expectations for new hires and training them adequately, and good ongoing communication.

I am not a very enthusiastic manager of people—I prefer to hire gifted self-starters and set them free. But some people, even if they are really talented, need more support and direction (especially very young people! Which is who we tend to hire). Knowing my own deficits, we have tasked our associate pastor with being the supervisor of most of the staff—it's a non-traditional way of structuring the staff, but he is good at it, it builds his role, and it works. Know your deficits and strengths, as well as those of your colleagues, and do what works!

As a staff without a single full-time employee, we don't see each other a lot in physical space. The worship staff meets and obviously sees each other in worship, the children's ministry staff connects in the course of their work, but we are very rarely all in the same space at the same time (even in our small-medium church, sometimes a couple of months have gone by without me meeting the new nursery caregiver, which is strange).

To counteract this "alienated roommate" syndrome we have an annual staff retreat at which we get to know each other, share our stories, clarify our roles and ask for the support we need, eat and worship together. It is only three hours long (you can't ask people who only work three hours/week to go away for the weekend with you!).

We also go out to dinner for a Christmas Party, every December, with our partners. We have a Facebook group where we can check in with each other. We could probably do better with communication, but what we do works pretty well. We're a happy crew, if a transient one, and our life together is sweet!

Leadership style and collaboration: Everybody *says* they work collaboratively, and at First Church Somerville we are no exception. But even though we are in a (flat-hierarchy) Congregational church, I am still the senior staff person, and the buck (and responsibility) stops with me. This kind of accountability and leadership is important for getting things done and moving the whole enterprise forward.

Shared space: We made sure, when we built a new office, that there was room for everybody in it: a long counter where people could do projects or plug in a laptop, wifi, mailbox for everyone on staff and standing committees and teams, copier/scanner and easily findable supplies, air conditioning and a small meeting area with new comfy chairs, as well as the church admin's desk that she generously lets anyone work at. I am ruthless about throwing away junk and making sure detritus gets back to its owners so that the office is tidy and calm, an oasis for anyone to move and work in, and a hub for church life.

We turned a large storage space inside the office into a tiny interior office that the associate pastor and I share (I also tend to work from home a lot, which helps with the work/family rhythms). That way, we are working closely together, which facilitates communication.

To help manage all the transitions, we have not only a crack church administrator, but a fully functional Personnel committee. They get new hires the right forms and keys, they execute contracts and job descriptions, they help the staff set goals, resolve conflicts and do exit interviews when staff move on.

A word about compensation: people are not going to get rich off of working at First Church Somerville, but we pay our people market rate or better for what they do. Even though working for a church as fun and flexible as ours is its own reward, we also believe that fair compensation is a justice issue. Something would be rotten at the core of our church if we underpaid people just because we could get away with it. In the Appendix you'll see a copy of our 2014 budget, including salaries.

ELECTRONICA

Fortunately for the Church, there are a million new electronic ways to communicate, do outreach and get our work done. Unfortunately for the Church, there are a million new ways to communicate, do outreach and get our work done!

Doubtless you are aware of and have mastered at least a couple of these, perhaps all of them. Here is a full complement of some of the programs, software and social media tools we use. Other people have written more and better about social media, so I'll keep it simple.

Email: Duh. We use email a lot—perhaps too much! We use it to do the bulk of our administrative work. I don't even know the phone numbers of a lot of our parishioners. That said, we are pretty savvy about not using email to do things email isn't good for: have a nuanced conversation, work through a conflict, have deeper discussion. There are times when email makes a project or conversation inefficient and leaders need to recognize it and cut it off!

I am careful, when I am emailing a parishioner about church work, to always, always first ask them about themselves, or reference something I know about them. Positive psychology shows this makes people more receptive to what you will say—and it just makes good, Christian sense to relate to the whole person and not just the job you want them to do for the church.

Listservs and Yahoogroups: We have one main listserv (on Yahoo Group) for the community. It's grown from about 30 members to about 250 members. At times, we have worried that it was generating too much traffic (everything from looking for cat-sitters, posting apartments, links to interesting community events) to be useful: we worried that people would tune out. But, for the most part, participation and the open rate have stayed strong.

We now have secondary listservs for affinity groups within the church: young adults, parents, and our prayer team, people who like to cook for life events (birth/illness/death), etc. This is the direction we are moving in: grouping people by interest and developing sublists to promote greater engagement.

I always, always (and encourage other staff and leaders to do this) write emails that are fun, upbeat, and concise. People should know from the first sentence what the point is. We all get a lot of email—don't waste people's time.

I also use emails to the community listserv as "pastoral letters" to reinforce culture I want to take hold, set expectations, generate enthusiasm and hope. Here's a "this week at First Church" email I wrote early on, before we went to weekly newsletter model, that demonstrates the kind of Doomsday Pollyanna tone of a church that is trying to pull up from the nosedive:

> Dear Sisters and Brothers in Christ,
>
> We have a full Sunday this week in worship and after: because we missed quorum at last week's budget meeting by a few numbers, we had to postpone it until this coming Sunday. In the meantime, we are getting quorum the hard way—by initiating 9 new members into the church! OK, so they were going to join anyhow. But I'm sure the prospect of full voting privileges tipped the scales for them.
>
> Please get ready to offer your warmest welcome to our newest members, whether they've been around for years or just months: Mary Alice, Liz, Patty, Roberta, Bill, Emilio, Peter, and, you know, like, me. Remember that coffee hour is intimidating

even for extroverts, and please go up and introduce yourself and find out what you have in common besides that you both have found a home at FCS.

I'll be preaching on the gifts our new members have to share in our community, drawing from Paul's elegant homily on the subject of spiritual gifts in First Letter to the Corinthians. We'll also celebrate communion as a way of cementing our Oneness in Christ.

. . . And just because we have nine more votes, please don't leave right after the service! We'd like everyone's input on some important projects coming to our church. We'll have you out in *plenty* of time to put on your blue facepaint. And since I can't say it during prayers (God being impartial and all), I'll say it now: Go Pats!

Blessings and peace,

Molly

Mailchimp: We no longer send a paper newsletter. For a while we moved from sending a monthly print newsletter to sending a quarterly newsletter, but then that quietly disappeared, and nobody seemed to miss it (I should say that of about 300 active participants and another 250 "alumni" in diaspora, we only have four elderly people left, two of whom are too ill to read anymore). Instead, we send a weekly e-newsletter via Mailchimp, which is easy to use and *free*. We send it on Thursday, and it highlights Sunday worship, our main event, with sidebar articles on other upcoming activities and the calendar for the week. This method works great for our short-attention-span congregation, which eschews RSVPs and embraces spontaneity.

Google Docs and Dropbox: We use both of these a lot to store and co-edit budget spreadsheets, bulletin information, meeting minutes. We print and use very little paper as a result. We physically archive almost nothing anymore—it's all in the Cloud. Google docs is great for spreadsheets, forms (like our Spiritual Gifts Inventory), databases (like our Currently Attending spreadsheet, with Sticky, Stuck and UnStuck tabs). Dropbox is useful for storing big files, like photos for the website, and we also use it to scan the guest cards and prayer cards that we receive from worship each week, so members of the prayer team and pastors can access them from wherever they are, instantly—*and* see prayer requests written in the requester's own hand, a powerful motivator to pray.

Doodle: I can't say enough good about Doodle, a web tool for scheduling meetings and events. It's simple to use, doesn't even require a login, and avoids the endless, dreadful email threads in which we try (and usually fail) to find the Perfect Time for the Meeting, by which time we're too exhausted to meet.

Survey Monkey: I have mixed feelings about Survey Monkey. It used to be great. Now it has gotten a little spammy, and complicated, and Google offers a "Forms" function that does the same thing. So, I'm migrating to Google forms. But if you are a bit of a technophobe you might find Survey Monkey easier to use.

Texting vs. phoning vs. email vs. in person: Again, you all probably have your own habits and wisdom on this. I came late to texting but am a full-on convert now. I find that most people don't really love to talk on the phone—and neither do I—reception can be poor, it can be hard to hear what the other person is saying, we miss non-verbal cues. When I am checking in with someone I don't know well, and want to leave a little more distance between us, I will email. When I am checking in with someone I know well, I will text (unless I know for a fact that they don't text or just prefer a phone call). If they need real pastoral care, nothing will do like the face to face. I go for a lot of walks with people (Exercise! Sunshine!) and also hold Office Hours.

Website: There is simply no excuse for not having a good, sophisticated, basic website these days. You don't need to hire a company to build you a professional website for thousands of dollars, though we just did.

Before that, we used a Wordpress blog template to build a quick and dirty "digital brochure" that was our website for many years. By "digital brochure" I meant that it wasn't terribly interactive or constantly fresh, but it gave people a fairly robust look inside our community. It had nice pictures, felt airy and open, and didn't have Times New Roman (blech!) anywhere on it.

At the very minimum your website should have some good pictures that show seekers what kind of people are in your church, tell them your worship time and what to expect when they walk in the door, how to reach the staff, and any current groups/events. (Please don't do a laundry list of everything you've ever done!
No false advertising. Tell the people exactly who you are, right now. More is not better.)

If you can manage it, it is a *really* good idea to post sermons on the website (but if you do it, do it consistently). It is an even better idea to post audio, especially in podcast form, on the website. We have a growing diaspora of listeners, both former First Churchers who moved away as well as people who stumbled upon us and participate from afar.

We have a members' intranet where we post things like the coffee hour and Sunday school schedules, safe church policy, pictorial directory, etc. It is not the most important thing on our website, but is pretty useful and another built-in timesaver, so people can get the information they need without coming to a pastor.

A welcome video is a *great idea*—especially for welcoming folks who have historically been mistreated by churches.

And most of all: make sure you monitor your language for

insider-speak, coded religious (or just church nerd) language, or overtones of depression or poor church-esteem (you know what I'm talking about! Don't apologize for who you are). And please, for the love of Pete, ban the words "special" and "fellowship" from your website. Also "busy." Also "covenant." I'd love to know your pet peeve church-code and swirly-talk words!

Social networking: It is virtually impossible to make your church viable with young adults without some kind of social networking presence (Facebook, Twitter, Pinterest, blogs, etc). That said, know what your capacity is. I think it's more important to be consistent than to go crazy trying to do everything and end up doing nothing well, or for very long.

We are listed on Yelp, the website for generating reviews of local businesses—used far and wide by young people and even older people. It was a slow start. It's tricky getting those first few reviews written, because the site algorithms "read" them correctly as insider reviews, since you will probably ask members to write them, and filter them out. But how do you get outsider reviews?

Have folks write (honest, specific) insider reviews, and be patient. The fact that you're listed at all on Yelp gives you an instant leg up—there won't be many other churches on there, so you may win by default!

Our church has a Facebook page. We post updates probably 10 times a week. We post a sermon nugget from the previous Sunday's sermon, we post pictures (people love pictures!) of big events and our renovation as it rolls out, and of special worship as we are setting it up (Christmas! Holy Week!) to get people excited. We post the weekly e-newsletter. We have a pretty decent following on Facebook for a church that doesn't try that hard, and some people "lurk" for a while on Facebook but eventually come to church—they can feel like they are getting to know us without taking a big emotional risk.

One thing Facebook is *great* for: wicked cheap ads before big events. It costs about $50 to get placement for, say, Christmas Eve Candlelight Carols in front of 10,000 of your neighbors, and it's super easy to do. Huge bang for the buck.

We also do a tiny bit with Twitter and Pinterest (we have a dedicated person who handles our Pinterest page and posts the most awesome stuff), and we have a Flickr group. But mostly the thing we do decently well is Facebook. We're also careful to cross-post things from Facebook to our listserv—because in spite of what Mark Zuckerberg would have you think, not *everybody* is on Facebook. Yet.

NECESSARY SKILL SET FOR PASTORING 98% OF OUR CHURCHES

1. Conflict resolution skills: Read Edwin Friedman's *Generation to Generation*. The primer for family systems theory!
2. Conflict resolution skills: read *Getting to Yes: Negotiating Agreement Without Giving In*. It's one of the primary texts for the Harvard Negotiation Project for a reason.
3. Conflict resolution skills: read *How Your Congregation Works* by Peter Steinke. It unmasks the toxic forces that keep churches from moving forward.
4. Facility in working through John Kotter's *8 Step Process for Leading Change*. It's brilliant, simple and it works! (www.kotterinternational.com/our-principles/changesteps)
5. Excellent non-anxious presence and self-differentiation skills (see numbers 1, 2, 3 and 4).
6. Mad skillz in talking about God to the Nones (e.g. people raised without organized religion, who don't understand theological jargon and have great B.S. detectors).
7. Excellent social networking skills, *or* access to people who love to post on Facebook, Twitter, Pinterest, Flickr and can build and

maintain a simple, clear, sophisticated website for the church. No church has a long future without this competency.

8. A sturdy systematic theology: should be able to handily answer, in a logical and compelling way, questions about: God, Jesus, theodicy, faith, doubt, the cross, heaven, hell, etc. If you aren't clear about your own ideas, how are they going to be? And then be willing to add, after your monologue: "But I'm open to different ideas!"
9. Competency in dealing with mentally ill people (especially: depression, suicidal depression, bipolar disorder, anxiety disorder, borderline personality disorder, and perhaps schizophrenia). Our churches attract mentally ill people—folks who are looking for stability, love and a place in the world. But they don't always know how to behave among us and it's up to us to establish a covenant for healthy relating—as well as to keep them, ourselves, and other members physically and emotionally safe.
10. Financial management, budget management—or an amazing volunteer or staff person who will do this for you and help keep you accountable.
11. A heart for people on the margins: they're the ones who need church the most, and also need to hear from you that they are really, really welcome—really.
12. Understanding of church size, and how power and programs and emotional processes work in churches of different sizes, and in your own church as it grows (or shrinks).
13. Doomsday Pollyanna outlook!

CHAPTER FIVE

Outreach and Social Justice

• • •

I often Ihear my pastor friends say they are more liberal than their congregations. That is not true of me, in hipster Somerville, where progressive politics are hard-coded into the DNA. But I am more religious than a lot of my congregation, and one thing I can offer them is an understanding of how their care for the poor, the environment, historically oppressed groups and others dovetails with the Gospels and the Way of Jesus. This way, their activism is grounded in something deeper and broader and more enduring than the feminist texts they read in college (however important those were and are!); they are fed for this work from deeper springs.

When I came to Somerville, despite the financial distress the congregation was in, there was a strong commitment to giving money away to local and global charitable organizations. What we did do together was a lot of reorganization, winnowing the list of recipients to just a few mission partners whose values closely aligned with ours (out went the Gideons, who won't allow women in leadership).

We met with leaders from all of the agencies we supported, invited them regularly to speak in worship and teach us about their work, and we look, at every opportunity, to support their work not just financially but with our sweat equity. To this day, we keep the list of groups we support small, and make sure we stay in real, dynamic relationships with them.

We also take a biennial mission trip to an orphanage in Colima, Mexico, that is a big part of our identity.

MISSION GIVING AS A PERCENTAGE OF INCOME

Every year for ten years, when budget time rolls around, we have increased the amount of money we give away. Most years we are able to increase the percentage of pledges we give away. Some years we only increase the dollar figure (since our pledges have gone up every year, the bottom line is, we give more money away even if we don't raise the percentage).

In 2013, we gave away 9% of our pledges to local agencies and the Casa San Jose orphanage, and we remitted 7% to our wider denomination for their work, including supporting missionaries and disaster relief around the globe.

There were a few years during our rebirth as a church when a fiscal conservative or two among us would note how much money we could save if we gave less (or none) away. Let me be clear that in all of these years, we ran a deficit budget. It may have seemed like foolishness that we would spend money we weren't taking in, eating deeper into our fairly meager (just under $200,000) endowment, while running $10, $20, even $40,000 deficits.

We finally passed a balanced budget last year, my tenth. But there was something critically important, spiritually vital, all those years to saying: whatever our own current financial situation, there are others in much greater need and peril, and as followers of Christ, we cannot forget them. God has blessed us richly, and continues to, and we are to pass the blessing on. Taking this strong stand on mission giving ignited us and unified us as a congregation—even the fiscal conservatives, who are, I dare say, as proud of our generosity as everybody else.

DEACON'S FUND

We have a deacon's fund, a second collection we take once a month on communion Sundays to help folks currently attending worship who are in need of a grant (usually $250-1,000) to help with rent, medical expenses, detox and sober house tuition, legal fees or other needs. This fund has never been exhausted, and provides the community with a source of satisfaction in living into the Christian principle of holding resources in common.

CARDS FOR BROKE PEOPLE

Our governor in Massachusetts, Deval Patrick, once told a story about his grandma. She said, "Don't call people 'the poor.' Call people broke. Broke is temporary." I try not to say "the poor" because it sounds like a sentence, like I'm putting people in a box, far away from those of us who can make ends meet. But someone who is broke, on the other hand, is a peer.

We live in a city, on a street where a lot of homeless and mentally ill folk live and dwell. They come by church a lot, to use the bathroom, sometimes the wi-fi, to get out of the elements. These are ways we can be church for them. They always ask for cash, which we don't—and won't—keep on hand, so as a workaround we developed a system in which we hand out gift cards, up to $20 per person, per month.

The cards are in $10 denominations and are good for the local supermarket, the MBTA (public transportation) or for gas. They have become very popular and the demand has increased a lot since we started the program. We spend about $2,000 out of our mission and justice budget each year on the cards, though the demand is much higher and we have to say no to some folks who come out after the monthly quota has been used up.

Sometimes broke folks come by on Sunday after worship, one of the designated times to get a card. We unfailingly invite them to eat with us at coffee hour, and invite them back to worship with us the following week. The vast majority don't. But some do, and their presence blesses us. When children and broke folks like your church, you are really doing Jesus right.

Another benefit to handing out the cards, besides being able to be true-ish to Jesus' dictum that we give to all who ask, is that our people feel really good about this form of giving, their pledge dollars going directly to the (temporarily) last, the least, the lost.

CHAPTER SIX

Outreach and Growth

• • •

This is *really* what you want to know about, right? What do we do to reach people, to snag 'em and keep 'em?

I want to be clear that *everything* we did (and do) falls into the category of outreach and growth—all of it. Especially scrubbing mold off the bathroom walls. You have to walk before you can run! But here's some of the more explicit outreach/evangelism we have done.

The main thing to remember is: look for the action in your community, and be in the middle of it. Plant yourself there, be visible, build relationships.

A PEOPLE FOR OTHERS: MAKING OUTSIDERS FEEL LIKE INSIDERS

Jesus said that those who lose their lives for his sake and for the sake of the gospel will find it. We take this teaching seriously. Fill in the blank: those who lose their pew, their place in the coffee hour line, their privileged time with the pastor, their role as the Only Extrovert in Church—they give up these privileges so that someone new can find their way in to their future church home.

Growing churches are churches that have learned that God intends for us to be a people for others. The church needs more than its pastor or senior lay leader to advocate for people who are not there yet. Enlist the opinion of relative newcomers often—have them speak to their experience of the process of assimilation—positive and negative—with the wider church leadership so that you can find out how you are doing, and what the obstacles to entry are.

I've suggested asking a trusted friend or colleague from outside the church—preferably someone who is not really familiar with church cultural, language and rituals—to attend worship as a 'mystery worshipper.' Ask your friend questions like: What was confusing? What feelings came up for you? When did you feel included/excluded? Did anything we did seem clubby or unintentionally exclusionary?

Be prepared for honest answers, and notice if you get defensive when you get negative feedback. This kind of criticism is wildly helpful—if you take it seriously, don't minimize or explain it away, and consider making changes.

One example of feedback: perhaps you will hear that the way community prayers are prayed made the visitor feel left out. What in your congregation might feel like a warm and cozy time to catch up on news, might feel to a newcomer like they are eavesdropping on an uncomfortably intimate moment, or are just plain left out of the conversation.

The message offered by your well-intentioned, close-knit congregation is, "Our prayers show others how much we love each other, how much we are like a family. Maybe we'll love *you* like this someday!" But the message received is probably quite different.

Let me ask you: Would you go to four or five parties in a row where the same people talked to each other about things they knew about, and while people said "Hi!" to you in a friendly way, nobody made an effort to explain or really include you in the conversation? After the first party or two, unless you are a mega–extrovert with a bulletproof ego, you would likely just stay home in your jammies.

There are ways to be intimate while also making outsiders feel like insiders. A skilled worship leader will, in sermon, prayers and announcements, give plenty of context, explain inside jokes in a way that doesn't kill the punchline, and otherwise bring everybody along.

That said, there are some structures—coffee hour, prayers of the people, passing of the peace—that are natural soft entry points for newbies. If these structures are too hard in your congregation (no matter how soft they *seem* to you), you might need to forego your own preferences for the others who are about to walk through your door.

CELEBRATE, CELEBRATE, CELEBRATE

Dying churches are often churches with low self-esteem. Your task as a leader is not to build up the church's self-esteem but to build up its God-esteem: its sense that God is guiding them and is a big stakeholder and participant in its life and future—their sense that God loves them and is hard at work, and visibly at work, among them.

I've said it elsewhere, but I think it bears repeating: celebrate every win, no matter how small (example: "Breaking news: we sent 50 jars of peanut butter to the food pantry this week, and there are only 30 of us in worship! God is good!"). Preach using real-life examples of good discipleship and radical welcome amongst the people in your church, to build up their God-esteem and make them feel confident about their faith community and its potential.

Use John Kotter's 6th principle for leading change, and use it early and often. Generate short-term wins, and then relentlessly communicate that win, so everybody knows it! (There is a difference between celebrating and gloating: celebrating gives God the glory.)

If you feel icky about celebrating, remember that you are not doing it to be self-congratulating, but so people who need a church like yours can find it, and so people who have already found your community can feel proud of it and stay motivated to do good, hard, radical ministry.

One way people in my church often celebrate is in the prayers of thanksgiving: they spontaneously give positive, specific feedback about the way their church has helped them, and it generates a virtuous cycle of blessing and God-esteem in our congregation.

Celebrating does not mean you don't acknowledge what's hard and broken about your church. It doesn't mean you don't name your growing edges, or how you have failed. Celebrating and truth-telling are not mutually exclusive! There are plenty of churches that can't acknowledge their frailties, and this unwillingness to be honest just further hollows out the church.

LOCATION, LOCATION, LOCATION: DEMOGRAPHIC DATA AND NEIGHBORHOOD MISSION WALKS

Pretty soon after I got to Somerville and we began to see some early growth, people got excited. Every once in a while someone would say, "we should start a youth group!" This was, naturally, the next step for a growing church, yes?

Maybe it was selfish, because I had just come off 15 years of part- and full-time youth ministry, but I did *not* want to start a youth group. I was tired of sleeping on floors and eating pizza and running group games and begging people to chaperone ski trips.

Thank goodness, I had some demographic data to back me up. Somerville is a very young city, but it's young with young adults, not with older kids and teens. Somerville actually has half the national average of teenagers. So it didn't make sense for us to start a youth group. There were very few youth! Those that were the right age were, generally speaking, already connected to a Catholic parish or had parents who had already made a quite deliberate decision, passively or actively, that they had no interest in church. I didn't see that changing.

What we *did* have in Somerville, among the unchurched and spiritually curious, were: young singles, new couples just starting out, and people with babies and toddlers. Upwards of 80% of Somerville residents don't own, but rent. People move in and out a *lot*—it is very transient, and hard to get connected. There is very little sense of community based on proximity and neighborhood: people meet through other means. The street we are on has a busy subway stop at the end of it: it's a commuter chute, thousands of people with their heads down, heading to their destination.

So, we let the demographics shape our priorities. We did our homework: our denomination had a contract with Percept at one time, which compiles demographic data, and now has a contract with Mission InSite. The Internet has some basic census data, but it's best to invest in more detailed data that a private outfit offers.

We read demographic data to find out who was among us. Read it carefully and share it widely in your congregation. If your congregation does not currently mirror the people living in your neighborhood, begin to preach about who else is around you—what their hopes and dreams are like. (And for goodness sake, *hire* somebody on staff who *does* look like the people you want to attract!)

We also gathered hyperlocal data by doing neighborhood walks *during* Church Council meetings. Before we did any "church business," we'd pair off, walk the neighborhood for 20 minutes. We would mostly be quiet and listen—paying attention to who was walking, riding or driving by, what they were doing. We might even sit in a café and eavesdrop on conversations, not to be nosy but to learn. We'd pray for the people we walked past. Then, we'd return to our meeting, and compare notes on what we heard and saw. It was marvelously helpful, as well as a deeply spiritual exercise. And way more fun than sitting in the church parlor talking about paper plates versus china.

As a result of our research, we started our annual block party, so neighbors could meet each other and form bonds quickly. We've run new mom groups at various times. We regularly hold meetings and gatherings at local cafes or pubs, because renters share tiny apartments with sometimes unfriendly roommates, and church turf can feel threatening (to people hurt by church in the past) or un-fun (no beer! fluorescent lighting! furnace malfunctioning!).

We've paid close attention to the zeitgeists and changes in temperature/culture in our city, and made sure we had a presence at significant street festivals (ArtBeat and Honk!fest) as well as raised our profile around other annual events (Open Studios public art event, the return of college students in the fall).

All along, we've looked for the next kind of folks God might want us to serve in a more explicit way. There wasn't a big pile of unchurched teenagers, but there were other waves of folks who are grateful now to have found our church. Some of our "demographics" include young lesbians just coming out, gay men struggling with depression, theatre people, alcoholics and addicts in recovery (and some alcoholics who aren't yet in recovery), queer and straight folks raised Christian fundamentalist who couldn't square their theology with their critical reasoning and their politics, interracial couples, adoptive families, preachers' kids, single moms, Unitarians or spiritual-but-not-religious folk curious about Jesus.

For each of these folks, when they've come, we've asked ourselves: "How does God want us to be church for them, and how can we open our doors even wider? What do they have to offer and teach us—and how can we make their gifts visible, how can we honor their presence among us?" One such example: when a very charismatic and wonderful recovering alcoholic came to worship with us, and became a leader, and taught us about the spiritual power of the twelve steps—not just for addicts, but for anyone on a spiritual path—we made the first Sunday of the month Recovery Sunday as well as communion Sunday. We preached one step of the twelve each month for a whole year—and had someone in recovery at the lectern as our liturgist, telling the story of God's grace in their recovery. It has encouraged other addicts to come to worship, as well as given many others in the pews valuable spiritual tools they wouldn't have otherwise come into contact with.

Before you can grow, you need to know who is in your neighborhood/town/region. You need to know what they're interested in, how they think, what they need—and particularly, what needs are not being met already.

JUST THEM EVENTS

Our church growth consultant drilled into us that we are not about us—we are about *them,* them being people who aren't at our church yet. Once we found out who they were, we needed to think about what they might need. "Your job is to be an asset to your neighborhood, and to let people who don't know you see you acting like Christians."

He *also* said that our "just them" events had to be organic to us—that is, if we determined that our mission field was made up of massive extroverts who wanted to boogie we shouldn't, say, throw a dance party for them if we were a church of introverts (which we actually were for a while). It would be awkward and painful.

We should look for natural affinities and work off of those. This is how our Block Party started, nine years ago. We live in a radically transient community where it is hard to meet your neighbors. So, in the fall, we rent a bouncy house, buy a bunch of burgers and dogs, haul our tables outside and have a block party. Sometimes there is live music, usually there is face painting, henna tattoos, and definitely grownup time in the bouncy house. It is a hoot, and fairly easy/cheap to execute. It has bought goodwill with our neighbors and become a soft entry point into worship for others new to the community.

Another Just Them event that has evolved from our mission and ministry is the Latin Foods and Local Brews fest, where people snack on food and drink donated by local restaurants and breweries, to raise money for the Mexican orphanage we support. We don't hold it at church, which doesn't permit alcohol, but we rent the local Arts Council venue. It nets over $10,000 annually for the orphanage and is something our community has become known for. We knew it would work because we live in a very young, sophisticated, foodie-oriented city.

HANDOFF EVENTS

Another thing our church growth coach drilled into us was the importance of handoff events. Don't put together a big event that draws dozens of new people to the community without having your next thing ready to tell them about. This is the hook: how outsiders see our churches not just as one-time fun for them but as a possible landing place and spiritual home. For example, we march in the Honk! Parade as a church, with our marching band and drag queens, and hand out flyers for our Drag Gospel Festival, which is the following week. Or, at the annual September block party, we'll have a flyer for our ReGathering Sunday worship and Sunday School registration event.

BLESSING OF THE ANIMALS

Some of our "just them" events are also for us, and even take the form of worship. Our annual Blessing of the Animals is just such a one. We hold it outside on the lawn, weather permitting, during our normal Sunday worship time. We invite people to bring their pets/animal companions, even stuffed animals to be blessed. We have a sound system, water and pet treats for the animals, and outdoor coffee hour afterward. We make sure to post it all over the place, including pet stores! It's a big hit.

DRAG GOSPEL FESTIVAL

Our signature "just them *and* us" event is our annual Drag Gospel Festival. The brainchild of a gay man in our congregation who had been to drag brunches with gospel music in secular club settings, he thought to himself: we can do that at church, and do it better. He also happens to be a drag queen himself, and fairly well–connected in the drag community—but it still took a while for the drag community to begin to trust us, a church, since Christian churches have historically been fairly hostile to them and their people.

Drag Gospel Festival takes this form: Saturday afternoon, a

talent show (not drag *per se,* but folks invited to be in drag) at a local restaurant-bar; Sunday morning, Sabbath worship, with our drag-queen-in-residence serving as our liturgist, our pastors preaching in drag (I keep it simple, with a pompadour and tie; our associate pastor, a man, has developed a full-on drag persona with hair and makeup and gown). The choir and congregation sing gospel music. It is not a spoof of worship, but real worship, with folks belly-laughing as well as crying their eyes out, knowing that the welcome is real and durable. The Holy Spirit is there and present.

After worship, we host a free delicious brunch, and have a drag show (mostly lip synched) in the sanctuary, with professional drag queens and kings from the wider community, and some home-grown. We have speakers from a local LGBT asylum group that supports queer asylum-seekers fleeing their home countries where they and their loved ones have been tortured and threatened with murder. The congregation is encouraged to dress up—in drag if they wish, in bling (hats, beads, boas) if they don't. The kids especially *love* this event—they get that they are going big for the Lord, and they are enthralled with the beauty and joy of the day.

We have gotten front-page *Boston Globe* coverage for this, and it's a great calling card to establish our credibility within the LGBT community as a truly welcoming church. And it's just a lot of fun.

LOGO AND BRANDING

When we first began to get serious about revitalizing our church, we understood that we would need to come up with a brand. If I just made you shudder, and you are already lining up your arguments for how we are a church and not a breakfast cereal, I hear you. *And* it is basic psychology. You can be righteous and above it all, or you can spend some time thinking about how people notice (or don't) your church, and strategizing accordingly so that people without a church home can get curious about yours, come, fall in love, and find a friend in Jesus.

We did this early in my tenure, when we were still pretty small and easily worn out, so we were going for a quick win/low-hanging fruit. For this reason, we didn't spend a year researching themes and focus-group-testing ideas. We picked a group of about six people who were really interested in/good at design and branding and social media (there wasn't a single person over 30 on that crew except for me).

We thought about the cross, and how much we love the cross as a symbol of Christianity, and also how much harm has been done to the "brand" of our faith in hateful hands. We didn't want to make up a name or a logo out of nothing, so we looked around our church. We have a gorgeous rose window that came to the church through one of our mergers—we used to be West Somerville Congregational Church, and when we merged with First Congregational Church in East Somerville fifty years ago, they brought their rose window, their name and their pastor.

Someone had the bright idea to use our window—which we deconstructed in the design to modernize it—as our logo.

At the center of the window is a dove, the symbol of the Holy Spirit. A lot of our spiritual seekers identify more readily with the dove than the cross as a marker of their spirituality, so we loved the idea of making that our central symbol. We played with the design, and ultimately decided on an eight-petaled flower, somewhat distressed, as a symbol of the world/Creation-slightly-tattered, and the dove entering from the side, God's engagement with the world.

We chose a medium blue and purple as our signature colors—fresh and lively without being overly feminine. (Lady pastors: you know I feel you. We are sisters in the struggle, in a still-male-dominated, sometimes wholly chauvinistic profession. But I have to ask you: have you emasculated your church in revenge? I ask because I see a lot of cursive fonts on a lot of websites. And pink! I mean really! It is hard enough for lay men to find their place in church these days without us raising up big pink barriers for them.)

We chose Whitney for our font. Again: clean, calming, fresh, modern. I made a rash decision to put our name in small caps, and am repenting at leisure, because our branding gurus in the congregation are very severe about this: once you decide on a logo and font, *Stick to It.* Don't change things every ten minutes to freshen things up, or out of laziness. People who don't know your community will only get to know it through repetition and reinforcement. If you want to get and stay on the radar, be consistent in your application (this includes all signage, website, ads, etc).

Last thing was our name. Our full name was First Congregational Church of Somerville, United Church of Christ. A mouthful, and a mouthful of coded, oblique language! Our national church had already discovered that they had an image and a naming problem. Even though we are over a million members, nobody has heard of us. If it rings a bell, they often confuse us with the Church of Christ, a very conservative Southern denomination.

And the name First Congregational Church of Somerville, while meaningful to local folks of an older generation, just didn't switch on any lightbulbs for younger folks. So we decided to start calling ourselves, unofficially, First Church Somerville UCC. We didn't take a vote, and we have never changed it legally (who cares what documents say?). But initially in conversation, and then eventually in print and in signage, we started calling ourselves First Church Somerville UCC, and it stuck.

We could have given ourselves an all-new name, but that would have been a radical break with the past for our older members who really cherish our history—and wouldn't ultimately have attracted any extra people, IMHO. So, consider reclaiming/recasting/repurposing when renewing rather than always dumping and starting from scratch!

COFFEE HOUR

Our church growth consultant Paul Nickerson said that visitors decide in the first five minutes if they will return to a church. That is not very long to make a good first impression!

It's not that I don't believe him, but I *also* believe the last five minutes is equally important—whenever that is. If that five minutes comes at the end of worship, when the visitor leaves because, 1) they can't find coffee hour, 2) nobody invited them to coffee hour, 3) somebody invited them to coffee hour but didn't go with them or, worst of all, 4) somebody invited them to coffee hour, brought them in the gate and then proceeded to ignore them to talk to their friends, well. You know *that* visitor is probably not coming back.

On the other hand, if their last five minutes is spent 1) getting warmly and authentically invited to coffee hour by someone who is not a paid professional but a peer, even if they're not ready to go, or 2) very briefly going to coffee hour where they make one or two nice connections or, 3) at the end of a really incredible hour-long conversation, sitting at a coffee hour table with friendly, interesting people, you know *that* visitor is hooked.

Lest you think #3 doesn't happen—I mean, who spends a whole hour at coffee hour?—it really does, all the time, at our church. Why?

It happens because we know we are competing, in our hip urban village, with brunch. So we serve really good coffee (Equal Exchange Fair Trade—we know our demographic!), with real cream, and tea. We serve really good food: we take food pretty seriously. We often call coffee hour "the second hour of worship," and our table is communion. If the table is sparse, it feels like the welcome is sparse, like the feast of God decided to grace some other place that day.

In the early church, communion was a full meal—in part, so that poor people would not go away hungry, and so that nobody could distinguish rich from poor. Our coffee hour is communion in this sense. We have tech execs and mentally ill homeless people in our congregation, and everybody is hungry after church, so we feed them.

In winter we often have a huge pot of soup, in summer, lots of salads (with veggies from our garden). We are nut-free for the safety of allergic kids (and adults) in our church. We are often vegan, in solidarity with the vegans and out of regard for our own health. We let people make what they like: one woman baked on-demand warm chocolate chip cookies every week for months. We love lemon squares and sushi, quinoa and lasagna and Oreos. We are equal-opportunity eaters.

How do we provide such a feast? It was always our way when we were a smaller church—we just loved to eat and feed one another. As we grew, it got harder to maintain the level of feastliness. So many people come to coffee hour, and it was intimidating to think about providing a decent repast for 80, 90, 140 people. It came down to the same few people cycling through, then burning out.

This past year, we developed a new system, called Coffee Klatches. We are still working out the kinks, but it is working pretty darn well. We divided the worshipping congregation of about 250 people (that is, people we see in worship at least once a month) into 13 groups, called klatches. We made sure there were reliable starters in each group, and not too many choir folk, parents of young kids, or others who have a hard time helping with coffee hour.

We assigned each klatch a month (13 groups=no group gets December every year, or August), and invited them to figure out amongst themselves how they will divide up the work. Ideally, everybody who is in attendance at church on a given Sunday from their klatch will pitch in, but some can and have divided up the month so they have intense responsibilities one Sunday and none the others.

People cook/clean/shop according to their income and ability. Some prefer to do all the shopping and not have to serve because they're chasing kids. Some people can't cook, so they buy cookies. Some are late sleepers but happy to stay till the bitter end to clean up.

In the 2.0 version that we are just starting (i.e. Year Two) we're doing some things a little differently. We are trying to send the message that it is really, really important for everyone to take a role in their klatches for the system to work, but that it is not mandatory (our Congregationalist congregation is allergic to hierarchy and hates mandatory—it goes deeply against our polity). We also do a lot of cheerleading/communicating up front now, including getting the klatch together at a special table at coffee hour the week before their month begins, so they can meet each other and begin to feel a sense of camaraderie and mutual responsibility, as well as learn the ropes of how the percolator and dishwasher work.

As year two launches, we are going to do a big group game at coffee hour (run by a church member whose job is to create custom games) to get people into their klatches and working together, to make those neural pathways.

We also have "klatch chaplains" that float through the kitchen every Sunday to notice if someone is alone, if someone needs help with appliances, etc, and to report back to a pastor if the klatch doesn't seem to be functioning that well.

It's our idealistic hope that the klatches, if not all then most, will begin to function like small groups—pods of people in closer relationships within the larger church where they can find both support and accountability. It's also an easy way to include newcomers, who want to feel involved and meet people but don't want to be on a committee.

GREETERS AND WELCOMERS

One thing we started doing early on was training dedicated greeters and welcomers. (See our training session in the Appendix.)

Greeters are extroverts or introverts who stand at the front door and say "Good morning!" in a friendly way to people just walking in the door. We say that the greeters are the "first face of God" for everyone coming to church that day.

If the person walking in seems confused or disoriented, the greeter will ask them if they need help finding the sanctuary, the bathroom or

Sunday school/nursery, and in general do a little traffic direction, preferably handing them off to another human being rather than just pointing the way. Greeters are assigned dates, and work on a rotation.

The welcomer training is more involved, taking about an hour. We ask people how they first came to the church, and what their experience was the first time. We ask them why they came back. Without exception, they say they came back a second time because they had made a connection, they were warmly welcomed, somebody used their name in conversation and remembered them.

We talk in welcomer training about the importance of getting the welcome "right"—neither too eager (the smell of desperation! creepy stalker!), nor too diffuse (yes, even in *our* church sometimes we just smile thinly at newcomers from afar and consider that "welcoming"). We talk about the fact that we want to grow not to make the church viable for ourselves—people will know if we just see them as warm bodies to pack pews—but we want to grow because there are people out there who need a place and a people like us (not to mention a relationship with God, but they can get that other places).

We talk about reading nonverbals, about asking newcomers about themselves (who doesn't love to talk about themselves?), about inviting people to coffee hour and offering to accompany them if they'd like to go. We talk about finding one other person at coffee hour they might have something in common with, and handing them off—preferably to another newcomer, who is also looking for relationships.

Welcomers don't have to be extroverts, but it sure helps. Welcomers are not on a rotation, but every time they are at church, they are in their role. We ask welcomers to look for newcomers before they spend time with their own friends in worship or at coffee hour—they understand that this is their ministry.

GUEST CARD

Every Sunday during announcements we say something like, "If you're new here we are *so glad* you are here! We would love to offer you our best welcome. One way we can know you better is if you come to coffee hour, to which you are warmly invited. Another way is if you fill out this guest card and put it in the offering plate when it comes by a little later in the service."

On the back of the guest card is a Prayer Request form—again, every week, we invite people to write prayers on the cards, however big or small, for our Prayer Team to pray through the week.

We use the guest cards to invite people to the listservs/e-newsletter list, to know when they are ready for a name tag, and to get their digits. It also gives us information about their needs and their gifts. You can see our Guest Card and Prayer Request form in the Appendix.

We have a Google doc spreadsheet called "Currently Attending" with three tabs: Stuck (regulars), Sticky (just got here; remains to be seen if they will stick) and UnStuck (people who have fallen away but we want to keep them on the radar just in case). We have a column on the spreadsheet for family/friends notes (so we can remember how people are connected) and "interested in..." where we fill in info from the guest card or from our conversation with them.

I used to write a snail mail thank you to everyone who gave us their street address, but it got exhausting and I gave up. Now I do an email follow-up where I thank them for coming, reference any connection we may have made, and invite them, based on what they are interested in, to get more deeply involved in the community at the pace that's right for them, as well as to let one of the pastors know if they have a particular need.

MUGGINGS

If someone leaves us their street address on the guest card and they live within two miles of the church, one of our members brings them a

First Church Somerville mug stuffed with hot chocolate or candies and a note that says "thanks for coming!" We are Yankees and not prone to effusiveness or proselytizing, so we usually just leave it on their front porch without ringing the bell. See? Evangelists have to be who they are, not who they're not—read the cultural context, and yourself.

THE IMPORTANCE OF NAMES

Remember them. I can't tell you how many times people have said to me, "I knew this was the church for me when I came back a second week, and you remembered my name."

Get names right in things like reports and on nametags and in emails/newsletters.

If someone has come to church two or three times, make them a nametag, even if they don't ask for it. They will be glad you did.

Encourage everyone at church to wear name tags *every week*. It is one little way outsiders become insiders. Nobody wants to ask someone for the third time what their name is—it's embarrassing. If people are wearing name tags, nobody has to.

Always have a good supply of "my name is . . . " stickers at the entrance to worship, on a highly visible, well-lit table with a table tent that says "Hi! Welcome! Please Make Yourself a Name Tag!" on it. It helps, a lot.

This is sensitive in the age of social media/privacy issues and a logistical challenge to catch everybody, but try to have an online pictorial directory or a picture wall in the church. We have tried to do this twice and failed (third time's the charm! Coming to a wall near you). But it is an easy way to let people do homework on names if they are not great memorizers (including you!) so that relationships can build.

I wouldn't bother with print pictorial directories anymore, à la Olan Mills—we did one a couple of years ago, for a gas, and it was one of the most annoying, ass-chapping tasks I have done in the last decade of ministry. The two companies doing them just have not adapted to the age of social media and technology.

Pastors, do yourselves a favor and develop this skill. Do brain games to help you memorize names. Use mnemonic devices. Develop your own tricks. When someone comes through the receiving line, ask them their name, or if they are wearing a name tag sticker, use their name in a sentence. Make sure you learn how to pronounce it. Nothing makes someone feel dumber than being called the wrong name, or the right name in a wrong way.

The awesome Christian writer and minister Fred Buechner says this about names, and his own name:

> It is my name. It is pronounced Beekner. If somebody mispronounces it in some foolish way, I have the feeling that what's foolish is me. If somebody forgets it, I feel that it is I who am forgotten. There's something about it that embarrasses me in just the same way that there's something about me that embarrasses me. I can't imagine myself with any other name: Held, say, or Merrill, or Hlavacek. If my name were different, I would be different. When I tell somebody my name, I have given him a hold over me that he didn't have before. If he calls it out, I stop, look, and listen whether I want to or not.
>
> In the book of Exodus, God tells Moses that God's name is Yahweh, and God hasn't had a peaceful moment since. (*Wishful Thinking*)

PARADES AND FESTIVALS

There is some festival or tradition (or, in our town, ten of them) that your village or city holds dear. Get in on the game. It's a great stage, a good way to become visible, to serve, to have fun and build cohesion internally. It's a great way to involve families/kids as well as people who maybe won't join a committee but want to get a little more involved.

We march in the annual Boston Pride parade and the Honk!fest festival of activist street bands. We have a table at the street festival

ArtBeat where we hand out free homemade popsicles on a hot day. We open our church as art viewing space for Somerville Open Studios, and more. We have all of our musical groups perform during PorchFest, in which people all over our city host live amateur and professional music groups on their porches one Saturday afternoon.

RED SOX FOR EVERYONE

Here is an easily replicable idea for your church *if* you are lucky enough to have a winning sports team in your neck of the woods (please forgive my unseemly crowing). In 2004, we were shocked and elated when the Red Sox finally got into the World Series. One of our amazing leaders who has a bit of expertise with A/V stuff decided to project the Red Sox games onto the side of the church, outdoors. We are in a high car-traffic and foot-traffic area, and also near a lot of bars *and* sober houses. Sober people can't go to bars to watch sports games in community, so we put out chairs, projected the livestreamed games onto the exterior wall of the church, and hung out.

All kinds of people came by: teenagers, neighbors, sober addicts, and church friends. It looked like the kingdom of God out there. And I think it gave us the winning edge we needed—that little wink from God.

OUTREACH TABLING

Three times a year we put a table in front of our church and hand out goodies to passersby to alert them that a significant worship service is coming up in our church. Before Christmas, Holy Week and Pride Sunday we hand out something appropriate to the season: hot cider and an ornament along with a schedule of services, rainbow cross-shaped lollipops for Pride, a flower or plastic Easter egg for Holy Week. We do it for about one to two hours on a Thursday, from 5:00 to 7:00 p.m., when traffic is heaviest.

We are on a heavily trafficked street with lots of pedestrians, and while it might seem terrifying to do this—and indeed, probably three out of four people ignore us—so many people over the years have come to us (eventually) because of our outreach tabling event.

It gives them a chance to see that *yes* this is really a church and not another condo conversion. It shows them what the people inside look like ("Hey! They look kind of like me!"). And it allows our neighbors to be "seen" as well.

Try to get younger and older kids to help! Kids *love* to do this (and drink five cups of hot cider while they're at it) and they definitely know how to soften up strangers and make you look "safe" and not like a bunch of cult followers.

NO INSIDER OR CODED LANGUAGE

I say this all the time, and you're probably already sick of me saying it: don't put any coded language (words like "narthex," "fellowship" or "deacons") on any of your outward-facing media. Period. It is a great spiritual exercise for us all to have to use ordinary human language to say what we mean instead of hiding in swirly church-talk/God-talk, or insider lingo. Be ruthless! If you're such an insider that you don't know what the coded language is anymore, ask your agnostic sibling or spouse or friend to vet it for you.

ADVERTISING

We have spent money on advertising in various formats over the years, and it was instructive. I'm not sure I'd do any of it again, though—just not a big enough return on investment. We have spent money on:

- AM radio
- Subway station ads
- Print ads in small and bigger local newspapers

The only ad I would pay for at this point is a Facebook ad, because it is so cheap and so targeted—*and* so easy to do.

We do also purchase "ads" in the gala programs for our local mission partners—like the homeless coalition and the Domestic Violence shelter, like the high school musical and the 5K. These often come for free with our financial support of their work, and it's a nice boost.

There are many other totally free forms of advertising, like blogging, having your pastor write a regular column for the local newspaper, writing op-eds in the local press in response to news that demands a spiritual or ethical response. Ye olde posters in coffee shops, LiveJournal, local community listservs (the Moms listserv in our town has 10,000 people on it! Free!) and group blogs, the scrolling marquee over the bank down the street, which posts messages for free as long as they are not explicitly religious in nature.

We print First Church T-shirts every so often, and sell them to members and friends—free advertisement, walking around town. We printed hundreds of reuseable grocery bags and give them away to members, as many as they like: more free advertising walking around town. It is very, very easy to make these things now thanks to the Interwebs (a great, easy T-shirt company to work with is CustomInk).

PASTOR AS COMMUNITY MINISTER

One big shift your community might have to make is in how it thinks of the role of the pastor. Does your church primarily view the pastor(s) as their personal chaplain? Would they be offended, or nod knowingly, if at coffee hour the pastor put a conversation with a veteran on hold in order to instead chat up a newcomer who was just sidling toward the door after being a wallflower?

The pastor of a growing church needs to spend a lot of time, not in their office or at lots of internal meetings, but out in the community: holding office hours at a local cafe, networking with community groups, and generally being visible as a community leader.

If you are a pastor, what groups or venues do you need to connect with to be more public in your role? If you are a lay leader, what tasks will you free your pastor from so they have more time to circulate in the wider community?

BEING AN ASSET TO YOUR COMMUNITY

An important phrase our church growth consultant drilled into us was our responsibility to be an asset to our community.

We struggling churches don't always have money to give, but we have two things that others in our communities who want to do good work badly need: organized people and space.

In our church we have let musicians visiting from out of town for a festival sleep in our parlor, donated space for mothers raising consciousness about climate change, nested new parents groups, fledgling community theatre companies, and college students doing community service.

When groups stay in or use our church, one of the pastors invariably goes and says "Thank you for coming! Thank you for bringing your positive energy into this space! And if you're looking for a church home, come and check us out on Sunday. We'd be delighted if you came."

We have lent out tables, chairs, our bullhorn, our pastors for blessings. We have sent people out to wrap presents for kids in shelters, direct traffic for 5k fundraisers, staff the phone bank for legislative change, paint youth group rooms for immigrant rights organizations, door knock for equal marriage and for immigrant voting rights. We are at the ready, for the right purposes, to serve.

CHAPTER SEVEN

Finance and Stewardship

• • •

Of course, finances factor hugely into the growth trajectory of a church. We were blessed by a couple of factors when I first got to First Church Somerville: we had enough money to do something, but not enough to do nothing. In other words, too little savings/endowment and you don't have any capital to do strategic growth spending. Too much, and you don't feel the sense of urgency that something must be done *now* to avert the inevitable decline and closure.

In 2003, when I came here, we had something just over a $200,000 endowment (it sounds like a lot, but it's not, in New England with an old building). We owned our building outright, as well as the nine bedroom parsonage next door, and a small outbuilding. We were running deficits of $30,000-50,000/year, and it was easy to do the math that unless something significantly changed, we would run out of money in about five years. We could sell the parsonage and live off of the proceeds for a bit, but that would only postpone the inevitable.

Our giving has more than quintupled since 2003; our pledges are over $250,000/year. Our expenses have grown, too, of course, but we passed a balanced budget for the first time this year. We are no longer dependent on grant funding (though it will always be welcome!), and rental income is important but doesn't make or break us. We give about 19% of our pledges right away, to our denomination and to local and global charities. In 2011, the last year for which I have data, we were 14th in giving to our state denominational body, although our city is 68th in per capita income for Massachusetts.

All this, in a congregation of mostly young people, many of them living on student loans or just getting established in their careers. Never tell young people what they can't do—they will give you exactly what you expect of them.

Here are the important things we did to transform our culture of giving.

MISSION GIVING

When congregations are in trouble financially, and people give in to the fear and depression and the myth of scarcity, one of the first things we do is protect our turf. We decide where we are going to cut our support, and that speaks directly to what we value and how our faith informs our giving.

Sometimes staff are the first cut made when a congregation gets worried about the financial bottom line. This is a different problem! But more often, the thing that gets cut first is mission giving—the money that goes back out the door to charities and to the wider church.

We have been very clear all along in our community that we would not cut charitable giving to help our own bottom line. We understood that the money we gave away—primarily to our local homeless coalition, our local domestic violence shelter, and to a Mexican orphanage that we have a strong mutual relationship with—was money that really relieved the suffering of some of God's most vulnerable people. We also understood, through the last recession, that lots of other dollars to those organizations were going away and not coming back.

So while it was tempting, and one or two of our more pragmatic members have made the case over the years that we could do more and better internally if we didn't give that money away, whenever they raised the issue it only strengthened our resolve to keep—and increase—our commitments.

Every year, our pledge total has gone up, and we have responded to this grace by increasing our mission giving. Sometimes we increased the percentage we give away, sometimes we kept the percentage the same but the dollar figure went up anyhow because pledges were higher. We all understand the theology of the tithe, and the idea that when God blesses you, you in turn are called to be a blessing to others. We are proud of our giving, and that creates a virtuous cycle that helps people be even better givers: not the myth of scarcity but the theology of abundance.

TRANSPARENCY IN GIVING

The single best thing I have read about creating a new culture of giving in church is the book *Not Your Parents' Offering Plate* by J. Clif Christopher. Some of what Christopher suggests may make you cringe and say "that would never work here!" Money is a very difficult subject—a source of a lot of shame and secrecy. Even in my own church they would much rather talk about sex than money! But it is a process. The more we practice, the better we get at it.

One of the most important pieces I took away from *Not Your Parents' Offering Plate* was the concept of promoting a culture of greater transparency in giving.

We spent a couple of years preparing the soil. In our deeply private, restrained New England Congregational tradition, money, and especially personal finances, was a taboo topic. We had lots of conversations at Church Council and Deacons about how our views about money were shaped by early family experiences. Many of us never talked about money in our families growing up, there were secrets and deep tensions around finances, and many of us inherited these old family patterns and anxiety around money.

When I arrived at First Church Somerville, the pastor did not know what the members of the church gave. This practice is very typical of New England Congregationalists. The only person who knew what was given was the Collector, the trusted lay person who takes the offering to the bank each week.

We talked about what it would mean if the pastors were privy to this knowledge: could we be trusted to keep confidentiality, to minister impartially to folks regardless of how much or little they gave? They tested their own assumptions, and more than one person finally said: well, I trust our pastors with so many other things—how is this really different? They minister impartially to the needs of kind people and obnoxious people—why not people of means and people with little, or generous people and skinflints?

We gradually widened the circle of people who knew we were going to make this shift, speaking about it as a tremendous spiritual growth opportunity. And when we were ready, we launched it. We added to our annual giving card (see Appendix) a box that folks could check. I had suggested that the box say, "It is all right to share my pledge amount with my pastor," but at the last minute our Collector said "I think it should be an opt out box, *not* an opt in box." To my surprise, the other lay leaders agreed—and that's what we did.

The box now reads, "Please do not share with my pastors my pledge amount." This way, people have to make a conscious decision *not* to share that information with us.

Very few people check the box: a handful of people, almost all of them older and longtime members who remember "the way it's always been done." I don't take it personally, and they don't seem to either. As for the newbies, they mostly assume the pastors have always known what is pledged.

I decided, when we launched this shift, that for the trust to be as durable as possible, it had to be mutual. And so, that first Sunday, when we handed out pledge cards, I disclosed what my husband and I give. My testimony is below. It was a weird Sunday! No one, not one person, mentioned it to me in the receiving line. To this day, I really don't know what they were thinking. But our giving went up tremendously that year, and the ice began to thaw around our spiritual relationship with money.

I wasn't the only one to disclose my giving. Every Sunday for the next three, a different person or family in our church stood up to make the invitation to offering, and gave a similar testimony to (1) the power of our church in their lives, (2) how they calculated their giving when they first started giving, and, (3) how they calculate their contribution now, and what the dollar amount is.

We make sure to have a variety of people offer testimony—not just DINKs (double income, no kids) but grad students, single people, even homeless folks! It is important for people to be able to see their peers, and know how their peers give: it gives them a sense of what's possible for themselves, and where to anchor.

A couple of lay stewardship narratives are also below. Enjoy, but please do not reproduce! Instead, light a fire under your own people—get them to tell their stories.

Rev. Molly Baskette, 38, married, two kids

> Today marks the beginning of our annual stewardship campaign, when we begin to plan our budget for the next year, and talk as a church about why it's important to give generously, so that we can do more of God's work, and do it better than we've done it before. As a church, we get a little rent money, and for one more year anyhow, we'll get a little grant money, but it's your willingness to share some of what you earn each week that makes this community tick.
>
> If you've been around First Church for a while, I might be the last person you expect to see standing here, as we begin the liturgy

of offering. You know that it's the non-minister-types who take on the task of inviting you to prayerfully consider your giving habits. This is effective—who better to hear it from than a peer? And that way, the minister gets to keep her hands clean, nodding and smiling from the fancy chair up on the chancel.

But the time has come for me to get into the fray. The leadership of our church has been talking for a couple of years now about promoting greater transparency and openness in our giving habits. We as a church are healthy in so many ways, and this is one way in which we can be even healthier: to relinquish the shame and secrecy about money and giving.

Each week during this campaign, a different person is going to stand up in front of you, and tell, as they always do, why they give. But this year, they are also going to tell you *what* they give. And I decided to go first.

I came to this decision with a little fear and trembling. What if, in your eyes, I give too little, and then I feel ashamed? What if, in your eyes, I give too much, and then *you* feel ashamed? But if we are going to get beyond shame entirely, we must move through it; and if I am going to ask you to be more open with me, then I need to be open with you.

My husband Peter and I give 10% of our take-home pay away. 5% of that goes every year to our church pledge, to the church that we love, First Church Somerville. This amounts to $80/week. The other 5% we have available for other charities we support, and for special projects the church wants to do outside of its regular budget, and for causes important to you, when you ask us for support.

Is it hard to do this? Well, it took a while to get to 10%. I liken it to taking a really, really hot bath. It hurts getting in, and you have to take your time, but once you're there, it's the most amazing feeling. C. S. Lewis said that Christians are called to give away so much that it pinches—that we can't do everything we'd like to do, because we've been so generous with others. Here's the thing: tithing, being able to say yes to Ian's cancer walk or to Sue's wheelchair mission or to buying equipment for our church children, has become what we like to do, what we *love* to do. As Christy Zuzelo says, don't give till it hurts—give till it feels good.

It feels so good that even though Peter has been unemployed since July, we have committed to fulfilling our pledge to the church for this year. We do this because we still have income coming in—severance, unemployment benefits—and to do otherwise would be a decision based in fear, not based in fact or in faith. We have also remembered First Church Somerville in our will, because, presuming we do not die before our children reach adulthood, they will not need our money to know that we loved them, and we want this church to transform our legacy into the kind of love that only a church can offer.

Why do we give? We give because God tells us to, because we know it's not ours to begin with. But we also give because we believe profoundly in the places and the people we are giving to: the inner-city church where I did my field education, which sends poor black teenagers to college every fall; the Mexican orphanage where every other year we fall in love all over again; and this place, this place that is so full of visionary people, loving people, servant people, changed people who cry when they talk about the place God now has in their hearts.

Peter's and my giving gets us into a lot of hot water, and we never want to get out. It feels too healing, too good, too right, to do otherwise.

Stewardship season has begun. The morning offering will now be taken.

Software engineering manager, single, age 48

A couple weeks ago, Molly told the story of the short tax collector who climbed a tree to see Jesus. She painted a picture of a man despised by his neighbors because he was short and ugly and he took money from them. "The tall, handsome, rich people never lack for friends," she said, and Ian Tosh turned to me in the choir.

"Is that true?" he asked.

A nice, modest Christian would have replied, "Gosh, how would I know," but I felt a surge of pride and said yes, it was. It pleased me to be thought of as rich.

But I was lying, in a couple different ways. To start with, I'm only sort of rich. I certainly don't come from money, and I don't have the savings I ought to have at my age. I made the strategic mistake of getting a PhD, you see, so now when I talk with a financial planner about retirement, they shake their heads sadly and offer me recipes for cat food casseroles. By one measure, though, I am definitely, if temporarily, rich. When my employer was purchased a year and a half ago, I got a "retention bonus" and a "stock grant" to be paid out over four years. These more than match my annual salary, so my total annual income puts me squarely in the top 1% of single taxpayers in the U.S. I stand in the uncomfortable position of publicly deploring the irresponsible Bush tax cuts for the rich, while quietly hoping that I might benefit from them for just a few more years.

There was another lie, too. I don't really know if rich people have lots of friends. Loneliness has been a central theme of my life, and is a key reason I am a part of FCS: I feel a little less lonely when I'm here, a little more known. And this is why I pledge to FCS: Money can't buy me love, but money can buy me church, and I definitely need my church.

How much, then, shall I give? My goal is to give 10% of my gross income to charity, but there are many people in the world in greater need than we are, so I give to a variety of charities. I don't anticipate that my income next year will be significantly larger than this year's; but I don't need any more, so I've decided to increase my pledge to $8,000 for the year.

However much you can afford to give or how little, you are welcome here. The offering will now be received.

Grad student, single, age 24

Good morning, good people! How are you? No, really, how *are!* you? Sorry! I quit Facebook a month ago and so I no longer see your status updates, wall posts, and zombie sheepvilles. In that way, I feel *disconnected.*

I can't find out about you for myself because I moved to New York City last year and am now a graduate student at Union Theological Seminary. It's my third school in as many years, having left Somerville and First Church after graduating from Tufts.

Such is the jumbled up life of the student, one marked by a multitude of loan documents and the inability to ever fully *check at the door* the demands of professors, students, reading assignments, and institutional life.

If that's the case, the question arises for me and perhaps for you: What am I doing *here!?* Why didn't I hit the alarm or head to the library this morning? The further question this stewardship season, on the day we go home with pledge cards, might be: how can I really pledge an amount of any real consequence?

So: *"why are you here?"* I started and kept coming to First Church because I sensed a spark of connection with this place: the justice work and values, the space, the preaching, the beloved community. And ! *gradually!* there ceased to be a groggy mental debate when my alarm went off at 9:40 on Sunday mornings. I lived close by. I came to church.

I came because as overfull as my student's life was, this place filled me in a way I had been missing. *I began to feel connected.* Coffee hour brownies were pressed into my hand, a soup supper was shaken together, my cup of fair trade coffee ran over as I sat and talked with new friends. My life seemed full, but I began to make room for this church, this community, *God's community.*

If you're here this morning, you already know how to make room, even if from 10 a.m. to 11:10 on Sundays, and you're gone before coffee hour. If you're here this morning and you sense this place fills you up, even if you're not sure how, then I call on you to make more room. It's stewardship season and our church needs you, too.

But *"how could you make a significant commitment?"* It's true, I know I can't give 80 or 100% a week to this church's bottom line, but I give ten percent because on a student budget, I *feel* ten percent a week. It leaves a hole in my pocket, and in my online statement, a hole that makes room for this church. 10% is more than $10 of my weekly pocket money, but much less than what salaried folks would call "take-home pay." At the start of every school year, I decide how much I get in loans from the federal government, and so I can't lose another $10 of my food budget or my rent money. I can give of what I keep for myself, though, and commit to something that makes room in my life for the good work of this community.

My small pledge supports our justice work and our outreach, but just as importantly, it *connects* me to that work, to this place, to you. A thoughtful commitment, one I can feel, connects me to you in a way that putting my spare change in the offering plate never could have.

Luke says in the verse that serves as our theme this year that "the measure you give will be the measure you get back." You go home with a pledge card today. Sit down with that card, a pen, and this verse in your mind.

The truth of that verse in my life is that from my time in Ball Square to my new home, a bus ride away in Brooklyn, my pledge to this church has connected me to the life and heart of this community and, through you, to God. Life is busy, but by committing to First Church I remember that I am *invested* in you, and you in me.

That is the power of the church, that is the power of our beloved community, that is the love of God, and that is the truth of the verse for me.

What is its truth for you? The morning offering will now be taken.

Married couple, no kids, age 27, grad student and graphic designer

We felt it was important to set aside money for church first (well, mostly) and actually plan for how much we wanted to give, and fit the rest of our budget around that, rather than just saying "ok, here's what we spend on rent and our car and eating out and whatever, and whatever's leftover, that's what we'll give to church." It took us a few years to make this shift, over which time we also were getting more involved in the community and realizing how important First Church was to our sense of belonging and our sense of home in the city.

But basically, we wanted to get ourselves to a place where giving to church was something we budgeted ahead of time, so that when the time came for big, permanent financial decisions like "how expensive a condo should we buy?" we could look at our income and budget and say, well, we want to give X to church so that means we have Y left over for a monthly mortgage payment.

And so this year we are pledging $5,800 to our church.

Epilogue: A few years later when we actually did buy a place, we really did think about it this way. I'm not saying we didn't ogle pricier places and consider buying them, or that we bought the bare minimum so that we could give more away, but our previous thinking about giving was a big factor in our discussions and ultimate decisions about how much to spend. If you had asked me several years ago whether I would consider my commitment to my church community as a significant factor in where I lived or what I bought, I would probably have said no, or not much. But I can't imagine saying that now.

TRANSPARENCY IN RECEIVING

The generation of people who automatically trust and join and give to institutions (not just churches but civic groups, etc.) is dying off. Younger generations want to know they are giving to organizations that are trustworthy and true, and have low overhead so are therefore good stewards of their resources.

Every year during stewardship season—as well as throughout the year—we strive to communicate to all of our people exactly what we spend their (well, God's, but from their hands and their labor) money on. We try to be profligate externally (e.g., mission giving) and frugal internally (supplies, stewardship of energy and other resources—without scrimping on salaries!).

I know this is deeply cultural—in some churches it is an expectation that the pastor will dress well and drive a nice car, as they represent the congregation to the entire community, and all share in that "wealth." But I believe, as a minister, that I should be modest in my habits of consumption. When our family needed to replace our car, I was careful to let people know that we bought used! I lose credibility if I am living at a level much higher than the people I serve, most of whom still struggle financially.

We also, during stewardship season, hand out a narrative budget or a Wordle (an online "word cloud" generator) or some other kind of visual or verbal (that is, non-numerical) depiction of what we spent our money on in the previous year, so there is strong communication of our values and our impact.

You can see one such (too long!) narrative budget in the Appendix, along with a Wordle we did the following year.

STEWARDSHIP MAILING

In addition to the in-worship stewardship testimonies, we mail out a stewardship packet each fall, as well as hand out the pledge card with a gift.

The mailing contains: an enthusiastic but authentic and non-jargony letter from the pastor describing in detail the vision for the year ahead (example below), a pledge card, the narrative budget and a custom letter from a lay person in the congregation. This is straight out of *Not Your Parent's Offering Plate.*

There are marked differences in how people give based on age and culture, so why would we expect one letter to encourage people to give as generously as they can? We divide our congregation into three groups:

1. Reliable Older Givers (likely elderly or Baby Boomers) are people who have been in the church forever, are going to give no matter what, and are probably not going to dramatically increase (or decrease) their pledge no matter what. They get a letter from someone in their group that says thanks so much. A perfect example, from our matriarch Dibbie, is below.

> November 6, 2011
>
> Dear Friends,
>
> When I meet people in church for the first time, they always ask me how long I've been here. I tell them that I joined the church in 1935 and I'm 88 years old. I've seen a lot of things come and go over the years, but we've always found ways to keep our church going.
>
> I have an old house and our church building is old and these structures need a lot of care. So won't you give as much as you

can to help us keep that "sweet, sweet feeling in this place"?

I want to leave a little something to the church when I go Home, but let's hope the government allows me to do so. Maybe you've thought about doing the same?

You can mail your pledge card back to Liz D, our collector, before November 20, when we'll bless it in worship.

Yours,
Dibbie

2. People under 50, who are already pledge reliably. They may have anchored a little low when they started to pledge—likely they don't give a percentage of their income yet, but some number they have calculated more arbitrarily. Choose one of your best givers and ask them to write a letter to them—disclosing, if they will, like the oral testimonies, the dollar amount they give and whether that is a percentage of their income. Have them tell a story! Stories are the best.

   Here's an example:

   November 1, 2012

   Dear First Church,

   Another stewardship season is here! As active friends and members of FCS, you and I have given our gifts of time, talent and money this past year and now is a chance to stop and consider what will we do in the year to come. The last 15 years, the time I've been at First Church, have been marked by almost endless transitions—joys and heartbreaks, accomplishments and setbacks, blessings and losses—and through it all First Church has remained a constant spiritual home. I know many of you call it home too.

   And what a dynamic home it is! So much has happened, *is*

happening in the life of First Church Somerville. You can feel it the minute you walk in – can't you? We have grown from being a small church where everyone knows everyone, to a medium bigger church where you can't possibly know everyone all of the time. For those of us who have been around a while this is wonderfully exciting and a little bit scary.

Then this past year the Capital Campaign was amazing! We as a church were asked to dig deep, really deep, and we did. Together with Jason, our pledge to the capital campaign has essentially doubled our regular annual giving. With the realities of home ownership and raising a family, these pledges feel like a s t r e t c h already. So what about next year? Can we really consider giving even more money? And what more can we give of our time, our energy?

Here's the thing: it would be so easy for me to rest a bit now and say—I've done enough, it's someone else's turn, I can't give any more here. But that's not true, is it?

I can increase my pledge. I can pack lunch more, buy less coffee, cancel cable, buy fewer apps, be a more organized shopper, etc., etc., etc. Will you join me in prayer and practice? Will you take another long hard look at personal finances, spending habits, and priorities, and see what more you can give to this place we call home, that is so constant when everything else is inconstant?

And what about time? What more can I give of time? Well, for starters, I've decided to sing in the Cantata for the first time!

How about you? What is the Spirit asking of you? Please, won't you listen carefully and respond bravely by pledging a bit more this year? We can trust the reward will be great.

Many blessings,
Sue Donnelly

3. Possible New Pledgers are new or newish to the church, and while they may put cash or checks in the plate they have not made a formal commitment during the annual appeal. Choose one of your most enthusiastic *new* pledgers from the previous year to write to them, and tell them how they knew it was time to put a ring on it.

   Here's an example:

   > Beloved,
   >
   > Welcome to Stewardship Season 2009, that hectic and confusing time when the movers and shakers of the church start tossing around mysterious, ominous words like "pledge" and "tithe." For a new arrival to the church, it can be a season of confusion, stress, and guilt. All around us, the older, wiser heads are nodding with the understanding grown from years of practice. They reach for their checkbooks and talk about these mysterious pledges and tithes, while we—the newbies—look around for an in-pew dictionary and drop things. Maybe if we just duck our heads and don't meet Molly's eyes, nobody will notice . . .
   >
   > I've been there. As a student, I avoided eye contact with those around me and mumbled excuses to myself as I waved off the offering plate like a pushy waiter. As a young professional, I hid my awkwardness by dropping a few dollars in the plate every week and passing it down. As a newlywed, I am still waiting for my name change to go through so I can order new checks and resume my offerings. There are lots of reasons why we don't give money to the church.
   >
   > This Stewardship Season, I am writing to you to tell you that you can afford to give. In fact, I believe that we, not just as a congregation but as a collection of individuals trying to make it through a recession together, can't afford *not* to.
   >
   > I grew up in Salt Lake City, Utah, the stronghold of the

Mormon Church. Now, their faith is in many ways different, but they have figured out that the most important part of community is the "unity" part. Every member in good standing is required to give 10% of their income to the church. 10%. Think about that. It's tithing in its purest form, and I don't know about you, but that's a scarily big number and makes me want to run in the opposite direction. But when a young mother died in our neighborhood, leaving a heartbroken father and three young children, it suddenly made sense. They were never destitute. They were never alone. The church filled their pantry. The congregation bought new school clothes for the children.

We at First Church do the same thing every day when we give money to the Casa San Jose, Centro Presente, and our other mission partners. When we give, we are not just standing beside them; we are standing with them. When we reach out to help others, we find unity with them. We become a community.

"Give, and it will be given to you," says Jesus in Luke 6:38. "A good measure, pressed down, shaken together, running over, will be put into your lap, for the measure you give will be the measure you get back." The Bible is full of promises like this, and it's very easy to pass them off as being figurative. If I give money to the church, it isn't going to end up back in my lap, right? Then I think about that word again: community. Unity. If I help my neighbor, doesn't that help me? If I give money that helps heat the sanctuary, I am reaping the reward directly when I settle into the pew on Sunday morning. If I help pay the salaries of our amazing pastors, then when I need them, they will be there. We can't afford *not* to maintain our community, especially now, when we need it, and each other, most.

So I challenge you to give, however irresponsible or awkward it may feel. Look at your paycheck. How much extra do you have when the bills have been paid? Figure out what you can spare . . . and then give a little bit more. It does not have to be 10%, but how about 1 or 2%? How much can you give? How much can you invest in your community? In our church, we must raise all of our own money, and our pledges make up the bulk of that amount. It is the only source of income that the church can truly rely on. When you pledge, you promise a certain amount of money to our First Church community. It's wonderful to toss a few dollars in the offering plate when you can, but your pledge is money that the community can count on to be there when the heating bill arrives. This is a year of homelessness, unemployment, struggle, and despair. Your gift is needed. I ask you, beloved: What better time to start?

Love,
Emily Deckenback

The stewardship packets go out in early November, and we invite people to bring their pledge card back two weeks later to be blessed in worship. And finally, the letter from me:

Stewardship Letter 2013

Beloved,

As I sit down to write this love letter to you, I'm six miles from Long Island Sound, with Hurricane Sandy bearing down on us. I'm here because our fabulous denomination, the United Church of Christ, sent me to a little inn, free of charge, on a six-day retreat as part of the Pastoral Excellence Program. They want to invest good money in good leaders so that good churches will continue to bring the Good News!

Church, the world needs as much good news as it can get. Anxiety has been running high for days, with new speculation about Sandy. Anxiety has been running high for months, with old speculation about Obama and Romney. Anxiety has been running high for years, with global climate change, the economy, fill-in-your-daily-disaster. What is a mere mortal to do, with so much uncertainty and so little control?

At the Democratic National Convention, Bill Clinton speechified that we weren't just voting for a president. He said we were voting for what kind of nation we want to live in.

But for Christians, it's so much bigger than that. Every day, by what we do (and by what we leave undone) we are "voting" not just for what kind of nation we want to live in, but what kind of cosmos we will live in. We are the Deciders!

What will we decide to do? How will we use our power to co-create, with God, a different kind of Kingdom on earth, here and now?

If you feel powerless, if you think you are too small to really make a difference, consider this: the median age of us First Churchers is (approximately) a youthful 31 years old. Two-thirds of our worshipping community has come in the last three years. Not exactly a recipe for capital campaigning. And yet when we ran the first capital campaign in living memory, we raised $620,000. We did that!

We also filled the sanctuary to the brim not two weeks ago. It wasn't Christmas. It wasn't Easter. It was Drag Gospel Festival, and everywhere you looked, there were newcomers with tears streaming down their faces, because they had never believed a church like ours existed. And now they were sitting in it. And laughing and crying and singing our heads off, we raised $4,200 for gay and lesbian asylum seekers from Jamaica, Uganda and Morocco. We did that!

I've long since learned not to keep artificially low expectations for our ragtag, transient, youthful, urban church family. You have defied the odds again and again. There's nothing we can't create together, if God wills it.

There's a storm coming, and her name's not Sandy. As we embark on a huge renovation, the likes of which our centenarian building has probably never seen, costs will likely exceed early estimates. We may need to consider converting some of our assets into cash to realize our vision of a warm, bright, functional church building for the 21st century. While we do this, we are also reaching toward fully funding Rev. Jeff's salary—not with our savings, but with our pledges.

Our steady growth over the last stretch of years, growth in spirit and members and dollars, will continue, but it won't be by accident or by default. We, the Body of Christ alive and well at 89 College Avenue, are the ones we've been waiting for.

If you can raise your pledge this year, do. If you haven't pledged before (and we are sending this letter to a whopping 48 newbies! Just think, if you all reply!), but you've found a spiritual home at First Church, consider making a commitment in any amount, so that we know we can depend on you, as we hope you know you can depend on us. We know this might be a scary step. We're asking you to do it anyhow—because we know how much good it has done us when we took it ourselves.

I've been checking weather.com and texting my far-off children anxiously all day, wondering what the storm would do, praying for those already grieving and wondering who would join their numbers, making the storm pure enemy.

But just now, compelled by a force beyond myself, I went out into the maelstrom. I stood in a clearing, the trees tall and wild and alive, encircling me. Not sheltering, not threatening. If anything, ignoring me while they had a deep conversation with their Creator.

My scalp tingled. I found myself weeping, for no good

reason. I haven't felt the presence of God that intensely in a while. I had been running from this thing I feared, but when I ran toward it instead, I found I was at the heart of things, and had nothing to fear. God is the ultimate non-anxious presence! The closer we get to Her, the more our own anxiety ebbs away.

Will you walk into the mystery, the maelstrom? Will you help us create a corner of the Kingdom, heaven on earth?

Christlove,

Molly

P.S. If you would like a holy friend to help you think out loud about how to make a decision about a pledge number, for the first time ever we have "stewardship confidantes." Six confidence-keeping, thoughtful, nonjudgmental people are available for one-on-one conversations, or as part of a more public forum on "how do I know what to give?" which will take place Sunday, November 11 after worship. Email Jeff for more information.

If you are interested in electronic giving, you can set it up through your own bank or we will help you set it up through Vanco services. Email our collector.

PLEDGE CARD

We hand out the pledge card (see a copy in the Appendix) with a small gift: not a plastic trinket or some other junk that will end up in a drawer, but something meaningful and homemade, usually food and often related to the theme of the stewardship campaign/the guiding scripture. We have handed out hot rolls stuffed with melting chocolate, bean soup packets, whoopee pies, et alia.

The most fun thing about our pledge card is the By The Numbers that graces the back—bullets that indicate in numbers the strength and vitality of our community. (See Appendix.)

ELECTRONIC GIVING

Just do it! Make it easy for people, invite them often to make the switch, and thank them for doing it. Tell them how much time and energy it saves, and how well it allows the church to plan for recurring and unexpected expenses.

The more people give electronically, the smoother the cash flow is, and the better people are (duh) at keeping up with their commitments to their church.

STEWARDSHIP CONFIDANTES

We know how much secrecy, shame and faulty thinking/bad theology is wrapped up in our relationship with money. So, last year we invited some of our most mature givers ("mature" meaning: not older, nor even the highest-giving, but people who knew how to think about and talk about faith and giving with ease and grace) to be Stewardship Confidantes.

We had an after-church opportunity for new givers to sit down with them and talk about confidentiality, fear and risk, and how the nexus between their faith and their finances had evolved over time. People could participate in the group conversation, and/or invite individual Confidantes to have a one-on-one conversation with them.

Confidantes are: committed, mature, nonjudgmental givers, usually laity. They are comfortable praying aloud with people, and understand the importance of keeping confidentiality.

LEVERAGING REAL ESTATE AND OTHER ASSETS

Probably you are pretty good at renting out your building—most churches are. But are you doing the very best you can by your real estate and other assets?

You can sell off bits if you need to, and you may have to, in order to invest in a radical new vision for growth. *But* there might be other things you can do, that will have a bigger long-term positive impact on your finances.

Three quick examples from our church:

- I inherited a giant nine-bedroom Victorian parsonage when I became First Church Somerville's solo pastor. Even living as I did with my mother in law, my father, my husband and our son (and later our daughter!), no way did we need that much space. My dad lived on the third floor rent-free and converted it at cost into a separate one-bedroom apartment. This could serve as a "second parsonage" for a second pastor, but we have rented it out for now, at market rent (which is considerable in our area), to a member of the church. He has his own private entrance. It paid for itself in three years and now we have a very reliable new income stream.
- We have an outbuilding with electricity but no heat or water that was full of old junk. We tossed the old junk, threw up an interior wall, and rent half to a theatre company to store their equipment and half to a sculptor for his studio. He has collaborated with us on several worship projects, and we can also borrow the theatre company's flats when we need to as a stage for various events!
- When my husband and I bought our home and moved out of the parsonage, the church briefly considered listing the pastor's unit on the open rental market. But we had a strong commitment to the recovery community, with some very active and skilled leaders within the congregation, and under their initiative have turned the downstairs unit of the parsonage into a private residential sober community for women. The women (or their grateful families) pay well below the going rate for such a facility, and even after other attendant expenses, the house earns more or less market rent. And, the relationship has spawned some important connections between the church and the recovery community.

GRANTS

A generous colleague clued me in to some grant funding sources that she was getting to support her own renewing church. Grant funding is not necessarily a reliable source of long-term income, but it can permit you to have a little fun and run start-up programs without much risk.

We have gotten grant funding from: local churches that closed but thoughtfully put the proceeds from their real estate into a legacy trust, state and national denominational bodies, the Lilly Foundation (great for sabbatical funds! Especially through the Louisville Institute), the local arts council and a local seminary.

CAPITAL CAMPAIGNS

I never thought we would be able to do a capital campaign, but our 101-year-old building necessitated it. Pieces of the church were literally falling off onto the street and onto people's heads inside the sanctuary during Sunday morning worship (talk about motivation!).

We thought about running one ourselves, because consultants took such a big bite of the proceeds, but ultimately decided it would pay for itself. We hired an experienced consultant (who ended up joining our church! But we still paid her) who led us through the process.

It was a lot of work, *and* very worth it. With a formal membership of only 135 people, and 250 currently attending, and a number of folks in diaspora who had moved away, and some generous parents of young adult congregants, we raised over $600,000 to fix our building envelope, renovate the sanctuary and make strategic improvements to infrastructure, like bathrooms, Sunday school space and the fellowship hall.

How did we manage to have such a successful capital campaign, largely from people without capital, but who live paycheck to paycheck? Basic, outsized gratitude, and a heavy buy-in to the vision. Their lives had been changed, they had met soul friends (and sometimes life's love), gotten sober, turned around their mental health, found their vocation, and more, because of their faith community and the God who guides us.

SPENDING MONEY TO GROW

I've said it before, and I'll say it again: throughout my tenure, we have allocated money every single year, often significant money, to growth efforts. At the very least, we allocated a budget (at least $2,000) every year for Outreach/Growth (signage, advertising, Just Them events, parties, mugs, T-shirts, grocery bags, et alia).

We spent money for additional staff: Sunday school teachers, increased admin hours, and, eventually (with grant funding for the first two years of the position), a half-time Minister of Outreach. We now have two almost full-time pastors for a worshipping congregation of nearly 300.

MINISTERS AND FINANCIAL GIVING

I have to say this, even though it will probably get me in trouble with some of my colleagues: as leaders of our congregation, we have to be out-front financial givers. That means: tithing. My husband and I tithe out of our net income after student loan payments: at least 5% to church and 5% to other charitable organizations (including our church's capital campaign).

Sometimes (yes, it's true—and I was one of them, at my previous church), ministers are among the worst givers in church—not that anyone would know except for the collector, but let's be honest: there's a Holy Spirit kind of knowing when the pastor has not put their money where their sermon is.

Laypeople, block your ears. Pastors, if you are reading this: we ought to be among the best givers in the congregation. I have heard testimony by younger, lower-earning members of my congregation about how much they gave, and it inspired me to step up and into my right place of giving—giving I could be proud of. As one of the lay members of my congregation preaches: "Don't give till it hurts. Give till it feels *good.*"

So many pastors suffer from a terrible affliction of workaholism that says, "But I give in so many other ways . . . ." If we say this, others will follow our lead. And the bottom line will bear it out. Do you really believe in the vision? If so, fund it—others will follow that lead, too. If you don't feel ready to give generously to your church, you might well ask yourself what you are doing there.

See the Appendix for two sermons on money.

CHAPTER EIGHT

Open and Affirming

• • •

Open and Affirming (ONA) is my denomination's code for "open to and affirming of gay, lesbian, bisexual, transgender and questioning peoples." I'm not interested in getting into a theological argument about homosexuality and Christianity. I'm assuming that you're on board with having LGBT folk at your church, and accepting them as full citizens in the kingdom of Heaven, with their God-given and beautiful expression of human sexuality. If you're not down with this, skip this section, and take what works for you from the rest of this manual.

If your congregation is thinking of starting the ONA process, which has educational, spiritual, and relational components, but there are members of your church who are afraid people will leave the church if it comes down to a vote, I am going to say this: yes, probably people will leave your church. Very few, if you do the process respectfully and at the right pace. There are lots of other churches out there that will be glad to have them, churches that support their point of view. And, if you become ONA and really live into your choice, many, many, many people will enter your church.

THE VOTE

Our church voted to become ONA in 1998—relatively early adopters. There was an aborted attempt to go through the process even earlier, in the late 80s—but the church was not ready. When the vote finally happened in 1998, it was in part because two very active and beloved members of the church came out during the process. Another critical moment was when the patriarch of the church, a blue-collar man in his 80s, spoke up in church council, and told a story about a former colleague, a fellow cop and all-around good guy, who also happened to be gay. Dick said something like, "He was a good cop, he loved to hunt and always brought me some venison after a good trip—*and* he was gay. I don't think there's anything wrong with that."

Having a powerful straight ally like that, the vote was all but assured. One family left the church. This all took place before I came, but, as I piece together the whole story of the life of our congregation, I strongly suspect that one family left because they were burned out after years of feeling like they were running everything at church, not because of the vote. The ONA issue just gave them the excuse and the exit velocity they had been subconsciously waiting for.

Becoming ONA is one of the very best things you can do to demonstrate that your church is compassionate, relevant and growth-minded.

THE FLAG

I came to First Church Somerville about five years after the ONA vote was taken. There was a smattering of LGBT folk in the church—maybe five, out of 80ish. One of the leaders in the church had undertaken, at her own expense, to have "an open and affirming congregation" painted on the outdoor church sign. But anyone who was not part of our denomination, that is, almost everybody who walked by the sign, would not have any idea what the coda meant.

I suggested, about four months into my tenure, that we hang up a rainbow pride flag in front of the church, as a nonverbal, unequivocal symbol of our stance on homosexuality and the Christian faith. I put it out there at a church council meeting, and let it marinate. I watched the young people look at the old people. I watched the old people think about it. There was not a visceral reaction, but some concern: "If we hang up a rainbow flag, will people think we're a gay church?"

"What does that mean: a gay church?" I asked, curious.

"A church that's just for gay people?"

"Well, I don't know. To me the flag stands for equal rights for all people, the joy of being exactly who God made you to be: gay or straight."

The conversation was not difficult, but it was a little fraught. Rather than belabor it, I said, "You know what? Let's go away and think about it and pray about it some more. We can talk about it again in a couple of months."

Well, the very next month, the Massachusetts Supreme Judicial Court decided to legalize marriage for same-sex couples. I went to City Hall in my robe and a stole and handed out business cards. Back at church, some folks made a big "open for business!" banner and brought a table out in front of church, from which they handed out sparkling cider and wedding favor bubbles.

Queer and straight, couples and singles: dozens and dozens of people stopped to take what we had to offer, and said, "I never thought there could be a church that cared about this issue—at least, care about and be on *this* side of it."

Our folks who had put up the table went back to church council the next month, brimming with enthusiasm and stories. "It's not just that the gay and lesbian people were excited—*everyone* was excited!"

You could feel the council loosen up. Maybe they had been worried about things changing too fast (uh, right—like that *ever* happens in an established church). Maybe they were worried about losing power if the demographics shifted too utterly (always part of the equation).

But whatever was holding them back, first one and then another older member of the church said, "Well, I guess we could try hanging out a rainbow flag. Maybe if we did it just part of the time—for Pride month—and hung up an Easter flag at Easter and a Christmas flag at Christmas and what have you."

And that's exactly what we did. Except, over the years, we got lazy about changing the flag out, and now we just fly the rainbow flag. And we are all, to a one, happy and proud to do so—because it has brought into the church dozens of people whom we love, queer and straight—and we can't imagine our church without them.

There was one majorish kerfuffle: an elder in the church died soon after the flag went up, and her son, who only attended church with his mother on Easter, all but ordered me to take the flag down for her funeral. If he had been respectful of me and our church and its culture, if he had acknowledged his very minor role in the ongoing life of our community, I might have considered it. But he was so rude to me, and so entitled, that I told him we put it up by a vote from the church council, and it represented something too important to our identity and welcome to take it down because it made one person unhappy. He came in the side door for the funeral. I haven't seen him since—but then, I don't expect I would have in any case.

THE WIDENING OF THE WELCOME

The flag was a huge help in making our welcome visible to all. But we had to back up that welcome with authentic commitments and follow-through.

Partly that meant making sure that queer people were adequately represented among our staff and leaders, by actively seeking them out and cultivating their leadership. Our worshipping congregation is about 35% gay and our leadership is close to that. The staff changes often, and in its current iteration does not represent our diversity in orientation, but staff structure is *so* important to setting the direction the church will grow in that whenever we are hiring for a new position we work hard to find and interview queer folks as well as people of color.

I am straight, married, with kids, so it's easy for other straight families to "see" themselves at our church. Same goes for people of color, queer folk, etc. They intuitively trust the institution when they see someone like themselves in leadership, as a pastor, music director, children's ministry coordinator.

Another hugely important step in making our welcome really real is making it audible as well as visible: every single week, in every season of worship, we start worship by saying:

Welcome to you if you are
Male or female or a little bit of each
Queer or straight or a little bit of each
Black or brown or white or a little bit of each
Old or young or a little bit of each
Rich or poor or a little bit of each
Doubting or believing or a little bit of each.

And from there we personalize the welcome for the day, having a little fun and riffing off the guiding scripture or the theme.

People never get tired of it. They tell me, wherever they fall on any of those spectrums, that they *need* to hear it every week.

One of our growing edges is: welcome to trans folks. Some have come over the years, and some have stayed—but lots have moved on. We have done workshops to teach us how to be more trans-friendly and to root out our own endemic transphobia. One place this has made itself felt is in pronouns for God in worship/inclusive language. I had gotten in the habit of using both He and She pronouns for God interchangeably in the service, sometimes within the same sentence. Likewise, in our hymns.

But some good folks on the cutting edge of trans rights taught me that even doing that, I was still reinforcing gender norms and the false binary of gender. That is, someone who is just coming out as trans may not be clear yet what their true gender is—and indeed, maybe never be "one or the other"—and so to hear only those two pronouns means they get lost in between, they're Nobody.

I have started saying "Siblings" or "Church" instead of "Brothers and Sisters" when addressing folks. I'm still not clear on a good pronoun for God, because for my people God has traditionally felt remote or absent so it's important for me to emphasize the personal, intimate, relational aspect of God—but I'm working on it.

Other ways we have widened our welcome: by marching in large numbers in the Boston Pride Parade, by demonstrating our commitment to queer rights canvassing for marriage equality in nearby states, holding a public prayer vigil on the eve of the SCOTUS decision on marriage equality, supporting groups like LGBT Asylum Task Force that offers asylum to queer folks fleeing torture or death in their home countries because of their sexual orientation, and, natch, Drag Gospel Festival which really put us on the map as a church that loves queer folk and knows how to have a good time.

CHAPTER NINE

Real Good Worship

• • •

There's no nice way to say it: all the growth efforts and expenditures don't mean a thing if your church's worship is boring or fake. *You* may have signed on to it, and remain committed to it because you get other things out of your relationship with the church (like friends, or privilege of place, or a paycheck), but here in the 21st century the church is competing with fascinating TED talks you can watch in your PJs and scrumptious brunch and lots of other sophisticated and fun choices for a Sunday morning or evening. Church is increasingly weird to young Americans—they don't know what it is and why they should go. What's in it for them?

You can argue that the attitude of the young Nones is consumeristic, selfish, entitled—maybe so. But they could argue that what we do is irrelevant and dreary, and they would also be right, a lot of the time. Why can't they get their spiritual needs met by going for a fall foliage hike with a local meetup, or make their confessions at one of the burgeoning public secular confession websites, or sing with the local community gospel choir?

There are still things the church does better, *when* we actually do them better: help people find their vocations, teach them about prayer that releases them from anxiety about the world and their lives, help them find people who will accompany them through big emotions and not shy away, among other things. And: help them feel that God is real, and deeply loves them, and is calling them to something much larger than themselves.

Here are some of the things we do at First Church Somerville in the realm of worship. Before I dive in, if I haven't said it enough elsewhere, everything you do in worship should be guided by two principles:

1. Be authentic, tell the truth, be vulnerable: interrogate yourself constantly, whether as preacher or liturgist or music director and ask yourself: is this the truth? The whole truth? Or just the way I wish things were?
2. Don't use swirly talk, a.k.a. theologikalspeak. If you are seminary-trained I know you spent a whole lot of money to learn how to write/talk/preach/pray like that, but if you don't use language that people understand, they're eating words they can't digest, most of the time. If you want to make them laugh and cry and feel and go out and be able to change their lives and other lives based on what they experienced in worship, use real, everyday language.

TESTIMONY

One of the most wonderful things about our church is our liturgist program. It was started by our previous pastor with support from a small but enthusiastic subset of laypeople.

This is how it works (full guidelines are in the Appendix):

Each Sunday, a layperson prepares original material for two of the pieces of the worship service: the confession/assurance of grace and the invitation to offering/blessing on the offering.

During the invitation to confession they tell a story from their own lives: about their own sin and struggle. It nearly always elicits appreciative laughter from people who share their experience, and very often tears as well (sometimes from the liturgist).

I encourage people to tell a story around which they have already begun to heal—as in Henri Nouwen's *Wounded Healer*. The wounded healer puts their stories into the service of others rather than eliciting so much anxiety and concern for themselves that the congregation is no longer ministered to but becomes the ministering.

The story builds to a climax, we join in the unison prayer of confession, then have time for silent confession before the assurance of grace and the sung response. The confession is closely related to the preacher's theme for the day. This is *not* an opportunity for the liturgist to monopolize the floor on a hot button issue or political perspective, or to do group therapy on "something they have been working on." In the assurance of grace, the denouement arrives: how God entered the story to save them, teach them, heal them, and offer grace to them (individual), and to all (universal). Here are a couple of good examples:

Nat

I have to confess that since early this week when Molly asked me to be liturgist, I've been totally obsessed with the prospect of my own failure—imagine a sort of Liturgist meltdown. "Perfect," you say, "because that's this week's theme! More evidence of God's work."

Invitation to Confession

Now is the time when we bring our own stories before God.

Today standing before you, I feel so blessed—an incredibly loving, supportive and just all around awesome (and growing!) family, good health, a growing business, and the love and acceptance of this community—but not long ago I was pretty near rock bottom. My marriage had failed, my business was failing, I was buried in debt. My best friend was a foxhound named Chester, who was dying of cancer. The only reason I got up each day was knowing I had to make breakfast and lunch for India and get her to school or I was going to lose her too. And she did leave every weekend to be with her mom. I was sad all the time. My life was empty—no love and no God.

A friend had been prodding me to get out, go listen to music and on one of those nights, I met Heather. (Truth is that she coveted the stool I was sitting on!) We dated, we broke up, we dated, we broke up . . . we dated and we broke up. Heather wanted commitment. Commitment? Living together? *Marriage?* Not for Nat! I'd been down that road and I ended up alone, betrayed, used, broken. The safe path, the only way for me to get through the day, was not to feel, not to cry, not to love.

Sometime during this journey, Heather invited me here to a service. There was a lamb. Hand drums. Rainbows. Molly and Laura Ruth. The Passing of the Peace. Heather and I went to brunch afterwards (Heather didn't do coffee hour in those days). We started having coffee together on Wednesday mornings. We attended another service together. We stayed for coffee hour. We got back together and I could feel the love but I resisted commitment—to Heather and to God—yet I couldn't erase the memory of passing the peace.

Assurance of Grace

The truth is that there was no epiphany, no miracle, no flash of light that suddenly showed me the way and some days I still fear the prospect of failure. But somewhere along the way, little cracks began to erode the wall of my indifference. Heather needed help changing the banners in the Sanctuary, a problem with the boiler, cracks (literally) in the ceiling. Subtle invitations, God saying, "Nat, the church needs you." Then less subtle—winter retreat, new member gatherings, buildings and grounds, capital campaign. And slowly, my fear of commitment, fear of failure, fear of love began to wash away.

On Memorial Day, Heather and I got married. It rained and

rained and rained! Like some kind of exclamation point—cleansing, rebirth, baptism. The most unbelievably special day filled with God's love and blessings. And any day now, with God's grace, we will welcome the newest member of the family.

Chelsea

Invitation to Confession

I confess that I have hated myself. As I gradually, begrudgingly, painfully realized that I was attracted to women and not men, I had to radically reassess how I viewed myself. I came from a tradition where all the adults I loved and respected taught, in no uncertain terms, that being gay was a choice, and a morally reprehensible one at that. It is hard and stressful for any of us to rearrange deeply embedded convictions. The process for me has included grief-filled years of journeying through denial, shame, paranoia/fear of exposure, desperation, and, quite recently, outward rejection by those whom I most sorely want to give me protection and unconditional love.

I'm not here to talk doom and gloom, though. I have not stayed in that place of despair, because hating ourselves is worse than useless, it is a kind of sin, too. The pain I have experienced thus far in life, the loss and rejection have given me perspective, have made me more compassionate, and stronger, and more mindful. Lest I make it sound like I've been a Zen superstar at this, let me clarify. I'm not. I've handled it really, really poorly at times. I have done it trippingly, falteringly, often gracelessly. But with baby steps, I have come more and more to peace with myself. I wouldn't have chosen to walk through these hurtful things, but I am soberly grateful for the emotional resilience this is all cultivating in me.

One of the things that has helped me is the love embodied in this church. When I think of all the churches telling gay people that they are despicable, unnatural abominations unto God, it hurts my heart.

Because this is a kind of spiritual violence. I want to do something about it! A lot of you were angry, too, when you heard about that North Carolinian preacher in the news recently, suggesting that queers be quarantined and left to die off. So how do we respond to violence? By reinventing ourselves. By building something better, more daring, more God-like.

The thing is, self-hatred just cannot be a force behind social change. Neither can hatred of others. I think one reason some Christians are afraid of homosexuality is that it threatens biblical inerrancy. I *understand.* I had to reassess everything *I* thought was true, and believe me, it was painful. But Christianity isn't a fragile vase that once broken apart and glued together can never be as strong. It is more like Legos! With these infinite and permutable opportunities for telling different stories, being creative, building up! And out!

We can respond to rejection with love. Rebuilding, closer to God. I think this is an easy thing to say, but is pretty much the hardest thing in the world to do.

Prayer of Confession

God, you made us in your image, and then, we confess, we tried to make you over into ours.

We think you resent, judge and hate all the same people we do.

Our worst selves long to have our prejudices corroborated, and so we gossip to the people like ourselves, and refuse to pray to You for our enemy's good.

Once upon a time, Your own angel opposed you, hoping to gain a power like yours. Since that day, we have not stopped following in his footsteps.

Forgive us. Help us to accept You and only You as our God, and to trust your ways. Call us into our best and highest selves, so that we can be peacemakers and agents of your radical hope and justice.

Assurance of Grace

To my surprise, some of my biggest supporters have been two conservative evangelical friends who are uncomfortable enough with homosexuality. Some people would call them homophobic, but in my time of great need, they have been nothing but gracious and loving. They respect me. They trust my love in God. They are grieved at the fact that I am in pain. They love me. And I love them. So in fact maybe they are homophobes. Even though their lack of enthusiasm for my sexual orientation is hurtful, I love them too much to draw lines in the sand. None of us are interested in talking about who is "right" or "wrong." And slowly I think we are challenging each other's assumptions.

These conservative friends and I are parsing out what it means to be friends, despite beliefs that hurt each other. They know that a house divided can't stand, and the love we have isn't worth losing. We're not getting any closer to God by counter-protesting Westboro Baptist or the very people who condemn us. Grace may come from directions where you least expect it. Don't close your heart to it, like hateful people do. Let's build our Lego-fort Christianity. I think love and beauty will speak for itself and other people are going to want to come and play.

It's also extremely powerful to have layfolks issue the invitation to offering, and bless it. Whenever I, as the pastor, do it, there's a strange sense that I'm singing for my supper. But when layfolks do it, they are peers asking their peers to do what they themselves are doing. They can be funny, and often hold their compadres much more accountable than we as clergy can.

About training and orientation: we don't have a formal orientation to be a liturgist. We tried that, but it felt kind of flat. People get oriented to how to be a liturgist by listening to other liturgists. I make an open invitation to the entire listserv once every cycle (about every 14 months) to join new liturgists. Few people sign up as a result of this, out of shyness. Then I make a calculated targeted invitation to 15-20 new people whom I think have the maturity to handle the role. They almost always say, "I'm scared, but I'll do it."

One important piece of the role: Liturgists email the preacher for that week a copy of their liturgy by Friday afternoon. We look it over, and help them edit: either clarify fuzzy ideas, cut for length by focusing the story, or, more often than not, make it clear what they're confessing to (this is not a chance to tell a nice, funny, or instructive story—it's a *confession,* which connotes the admission of a transgression). We push people on this, gently but firmly.

Sometimes I have had people do as many as three rewrites—and they have thanked me for it later. One parishioner likened it to "the most intense therapy I've ever done." It's amazing the spiritual maturity that can happen, in the space of a few days, for someone who has taken the courageous step to articulate their story and tell it in front of their entire faith community.

PRAYERS OF THE PEOPLE

We've gone through lots of iterations of pastoral prayer/prayers of the people. We've done all kinds of things that don't work, and that's how we've arrived at the model we have—which doesn't work perfectly, but is pretty darn good, and, lots of the time, extraordinary.

Here were a few of our early missteps, that I've given silly names:
The Mediocre MLK: a.k.a., the "pastoral prayer." I was the full-time associate pastor at my previous church, and jealously guarded the pastoral prayer as my "office" since I only got to preach once a month. I spent hours crafting it each Saturday night—speaking to God for the people, who thought (or whom I thought!) couldn't speak to God themselves. My prayers were nice, cogent, with great heaping mounds

of swirly talk and excellent extended metaphors.

With pastoral prayers comes a sense that the pastor is really the professional pray-er. That's a practice that undermines the laity, keeping them spiritually stunted.

The Merv Griffin: Our first attempt to return the prayers to the people meant I would walk around the room with a microphone. Anyone who wanted to lift up a prayer petition could, but there was a time lag between when their hand went up and how fast I could get there, with my vestments all aflutter. And, when they did pray, it was hard for it not to sound like they were on a second-rate talk show—not because of their lack of earnestness, but because of the general lumpiness of this form for prayer.

Also, once they heard the sound of their voices, some people wouldn't give the microphone back. We had two sermons on those Sundays.

The Echo Chamber: From the Merv Griffin we moved to the Echo Chamber: anyone could lift up a prayer request, and the pastor, miked, would echo it from the front. This caused unnecessary distress for the pastor, and embarrassment for the petitioner, when the pastor inevitably misheard the original petition and repeated it wrong, or didn't hear it at all. Ouch!

Also, this practice made the prayers twice as long. Which is not a bad thing, but our prayers are already about 10-15 minutes long, and here is where the law of diminishing returns is heavily implied.

Prayer in Three Moments: This is the way we do it now. We wanted our prayers to be really prayerful—we wanted to feel like we were really *praying* instead of delivering a letter to Congress, or giving God a to-do list. This meant we had to pray in our own language, and have a form for prayer that helped us go deep and broad, not just rehearsing our same prayer for Aunt Edna's bunions or world peace.

A good form for prayer would nudge us to lift prayers to God, calling God by name, to dig deep, and to send our spirits out, thinking about and evoking steadfast love not just for our own circle but for all God's children.

When we began this form, we prayed in four moments: *first* for the world, *second* for ourselves and those we loved—this was intentional, to train ourselves to, in fact, think of faraway countries, and big broad issues that affect all of Creation, first. To give them primacy. As people got better and better at giving their soulful, prayerful attention to, say, Syria, or children living in institutions, or alcoholics and addicts looking for a solution, or global climate change, we collapsed those first two moments of prayer into one.

What's extraordinary about our current form is that there is a sense that people are really praying. They feel empowered to pray, they feel that God has drawn near to them and that they have drawn near to God. They feel that their words and spirit have made a difference, substantively. They are moved to tears, or laughter, in prayer. They feel that their burdens are lifted. They experience an answer to our corporate prayers, and carry those stories of answered prayer back to us, their community.

Now, our prayers are prayers of the people, by the people, and for the people—and the world. Here's what the pastors say pretty much every Sunday at our church:

At First Church Somerville, we pray in three moments:

> In the first moment, we pray for the world, for ourselves, and for those we love—prayers of longing for the wounded places and people of the world.
>
> In the second moment, we pray thanksgiving for all the blessings of this life—because to name our gratitude is to feel more grateful, and because both gratitude and joy are infectious, our pew-mates will catch it.

> In the third moment of prayer, we pray the prayer Jesus taught them, when his disciples asked him, "How shall we pray?" The prayer known as the Lord's Prayer.
>
> You are invited to be *loud* when you pray, so your neighbors can hear you and so your prayer will echo in our hearts all week long.
>
> You are invited to be *quiet* when you pray, if that's your spirit's volume today.

The whole time we pray, we sing. Then the prayer leader offers some kind of thematic segue into the prayers, riffing off of the theme for the day and just *how* prayer extends or supports that theme.

People are invited to pray for, and do indeed pray for, everything from the ridiculous to the sublime: the cardinal that visits their bird feeder, bouncy houses, bubble baths, the double rainbow over the church after the thunderstorm, the end of chemo, the prodigal return home. No prayer too big or too small, is our motto.

When we started praying this way, we had some "plants"—people who could reliably be counted on to pray out loud and strong.

These days, some people have developed their unique prayer petition: such as a scientist who every Sunday prays for "swift action on global climate change," or the mission trip veteran who now names a different set of Mexican orphans in his petition each Sunday, in English and in Spanish, "Para Lupe, Chava, Regina, Chuy, y para todos los niños/for all the children of the Casa San Jose orphanage."

Even sweeter? When those two are absent from worship, someone else will pick up and pray their prayer.

A word about blessing during the prayers: in our very transient congregation, someone is always leaving. We used to do a whole little ceremony for each one, a blessing and sending, but there are just too many coming and going these days. Now when there is a person transitioning away, we do a fourth moment of prayer, in which we pray aloud where they are going and the calling to which God calls them, thank them for their service, and have the entire congregation raise their pre-warmed blessing hands over them.

A word about the music: We sing the same sung response for between one to six months. Our accompanist plays the song quietly while people are actually lifting up their prayer petitions, and at the end of each section, the prayer leader says, "Lord, in Your mercy" (after prayers of longing) or "Lord, for Your blessings" (after prayers of thanksgiving), after which the accompanist increases the volume and plays us through the response, which moves us into the next moment of prayer.

We sing for several reasons: when you sing, you pray twice. Music is a booster—it helps deliver the spirit of prayer into our souls. It covers the sound of tears and other emotion for vulnerable people. And it emboldens people who would never speak up into true silence. It mitigates the awkwardness when two people pray out loud at once, interrupting each other. In short, it works—with the right songs.

We tried not singing—a person or two felt the music was a little emotionally manipulative. But then people were scared to raise their voices. And we just missed the music! Even the people who felt it was emotionally manipulative came around (rubs hands wickedly . . .).

MULTIRACIAL, MULTICULTURAL WORSHIP

I did my entire sabbatical project in 2009 on multiracial worship. I visited churches that were exceptionally racially diverse, all over the country, and interviewed their staff. I read countless books. We have tried to employ some practices to lean into becoming a more multiracial church, but with about 15% people of color in our church, we have pretty far to go. (I sometimes think it would be a lot easier if we were theologically more conservative!)

One absolute must to becoming a more multiracial community is valuing different cultural expressions in worship. Extended, spontaneous time of prayer; music that employs lots of different genres and instruments; preaching without a manuscript or employing call and response—all these matter toward making worship attractive to people who likely grew up in more heart-led worship settings.

This year we have instituted a Beloved Community Sunday once a month: we preach or liturgize about some aspect of race, white privilege, and what it means and looks like to tear down barriers to becoming a church that looks more like the Kingdom of Heaven. Our music is always culturally eclectic, but on BC Sundays we make a special effort to lift up the cultures represented by the people of color in the pews. We invite people of color to preach, and thus lean into our vision.

Also, I can't state enough: the congregation will pattern themselves after the leadership. If you want a multiracial congregation, you need a multiracial staff.

SCRIPTURE AND EXEGESIS

Most folks in our congregation are self-designated Bible babies. We have a posse of people raised evangelical, but most of our folks were raised Catholic, mainline Protestant or Nones. You know what that means: with the exception of a few outliers, they don't know the Bible—or they don't remember what they learned growing up.

For that reason, we don't assume prior knowledge when we read and talk about scripture in worship, and we give a little context for the reading to prime the reader to hear, understand, and feel themselves more of an expert. This also takes some of the weight out of the sermon and doesn't "bury the lead." But we also take care to do this in a way that doesn't dumb things down for the really knowledgeable folk in the pews.

When we read scripture, we might say something like, "Today's scripture reading is from the Gospels, of which there are four. You know them: Matthew, Mark, Luke, John. Luke's was probably written down in the 70s AD, about the same time as Matthew's, and well before John's. Remember that Luke loved the poor: as evidenced in his Nativity story, which invited the shepherds and not the wise ones, the educated nobility.

In today's story, sometimes called the Parable of Lazarus and the Rich Man, you'll hear more of that love of the poor. And a mere two chapters later, we overhear one of Jesus' most famous dictums, 'it is easier for a camel to go through the eye of a needle, than for a rich one to enter heaven.'"

We don't stick to one translation, but hop around, often using the NRSV, the NIV, The Inclusive Bible or *The Message,* and even have a self-styled Inclusivist who happily inclusivizes the language for us each week, unless we have a reason for wanting to stick with the original text.

SERMON SERIES

We will often organize our preaching into sermon series. We've done Simple Shifts (e.g. from Isolation to Community), Seven Deadly Sins, Prayer, Summer Reading, Sex, Dying Well, Mistakes. This helps us to really go deep into one idea, exploring it from a lot of angles, and letting different preachers at it. It's made me a better preacher and helps me to organize my thoughts and think farther ahead.

HOT BUTTONS

By all means, preach on hot buttons! It's what people really think about and really talk about in the rest of their lives, and they need to hear what their pastors and their fellow pew-sitters also really think about war, partisan politics, abortion, pornography, addiction, adultery, polyamory, euthanasia, materialism. And money money money!

If they don't hear what Jesus has to teach about it, they will let themselves be guided and persuaded by secular culture. Don't they deserve to know? Shouldn't we have the courage to be frank, given how much is at stake?

By all means, know your audience—push them, challenge them, but don't belittle or demean them. Start from where they are, and move from there, but also don't play it safe—what's the point of that?

Have a "sermon digestion" table at coffee hour so that folks can play with the ideas presented in the sermon, and push back against the preacher in a healthy setting, and teach each other. We also have a lay-led bible study every Tuesday evening that digests the sermon themes from the Sunday before.

There's a sermon I did on sex in the Appendix, if you want an example. And, by the way, the most controversial sermon I ever preached? On whether or not to keep the American flag in the front of the sanctuary. Somebody walked out in the middle of it! They didn't even get to hear how it ended . . . and yes, we still have an American flag at the front of the sanctuary. One of these decades. . . .

PREACHING

I spend less time on sermons than I used to, because I have more experience, and I know exactly how hard I need to work to make a sermon reasonably good. That said, I think sermons deserve our very best attention, and we ought to regularly sharpen our preaching skills.

This doesn't mean we should hide in our pastor's study from all the other demands of ministry. It ain't the 1950s anymore, except in a few suburban enclaves, and that way of ministry just isn't gonna fly.

There is so much that people can be reading/listening to in our culture of Podcast Spotify Pandora super-saturated cable TV lineup, it is nothing short of a miracle that every Sunday, a whole pile of people are willing to sit and listen to just me talk, in real time, and give the sermon as close as they can get to their full attention.

I need to say something *worthy* of that attention. I need to say something they won't get from the *New York Times* or Salon or HuffPost. I need to give them, not information, but hope. And spiritual homework. They crave it, whether they know it or not (but most of them do know it).

So, every time I write a sermon, I vet it for swirly talk: am I hiding in Big Concepts? Am I throwing around theological jargon? We all learned it in seminary—Rev., I'm talking to you—and it's *so much easier* to talk that way than to say something real, am I right?

Here's a real bit from one of my early sermons, before I really started working hard to shed the swirly talk:

> To those who trust in God, even the darkness is like light. We gather together on the journey of faith, guided by the Light of God's goodness, providence and wisdom. We know that the Christ, the Risen Son, will guide our way if only we have the vision to see, to act, to be changed by the power of the Resurrection. Let us gather ourselves in love, bringing our whole hearts and minds to worship anew the One who made us and sustains us. Amen.

When you preach, talk the way you talk in real life, but *bigger,* more dramatic, to be worthy of the pulpit you are standing behind and the Good News that needs amplification. Unity minister Marianne Williamson said, "Our deepest fear is not that we are inadequate. Our deepest fear is that we are powerful beyond measure. It is our Light, not our Darkness, that most frightens us."

I always remember this when I climb into the pulpit: it behooves me—not for my ego's sake, but for the sake of people dying of spiritual thirst—to bring that God-given power in as big a way as I can.

The other thing I do when I am preparing a sermon is ask myself, Is it true? Am I saying something that is really true, and will others immediately recognize it as true, also? Held up against real, everyday life, not life the way we want it to be but life the way it is, is *this* true? And even if it's Saturday night or Sunday morning, if I'm saying something not true, I have to start over.

If you're going to preach, people: say something true. Say something real. Say something relevant. Tell good stories—true stories, not canned Sermon Illustrations. And, if it's in your gifts, make people laugh, and make people cry. Not to manipulate, but because it's cathartic—and we all need to feel our feelings, in a safe setting—because feeling too much Out There can be very scary. It's one thing that real good church does that hardly any TED talk can do. Help us feel something really human, help us to identify something true, *while* we're all sitting there together.

I used to really stress about the beginnings of sermons. I thought I had to say something unique, ingenious or clever. Then I heard somewhere: start with the scripture text. People crave it. They really want to know the stories and wisdom. So that's what I almost always do now. And it works!

As I said, I don't spend as long as I used to on the sermon. In my early preaching days, it wouldn't be unusual for me to spend twenty hours on one sermon. I would end up with about twenty pages of text—not all of it preached, don't worry—before I was done!

Now I start on Tuesday with notes for the rest of the worship team to see and riff off of, but I don't usually finish the final manuscript till Sunday morning. I spend more time thinking than writing. Exegesis and writing time = about five or six hours. Thinking time = all the time between Tuesday and Sunday.

I almost always do a manuscript, but preach only from notes or memory on most All Ages worship Sundays. I wish I were a better extemporaneous preacher, and I do it regularly just so those skills won't totally atrophy. My favorite preaching role models say we should preach in different modes with regularity, so we don't get stale.

The very best preacher I know is Fred Craddock. If you can get to a workshop of his, *do.* (*Nota bene:* he is getting older . . . run don't walk!) He told us once to write down one-page stories of everything. Keep a file. Don't assign the story a title or theme—just let it be what it is. Someday it will find you again, at the right time. When you walk around with an imaginary video camera on your shoulder, you will start seeing one-page stories everywhere—and you will not be a character in any of them.

If you can't go see him, buy the CD of one of his preaching workshops, *Thirteen Ways to End a Sermon* (which, he cautions, does not mean end your sermon 13 times).

And finally, a bit of writing advice from Saint Anne Lamott that pertains to preaching as well: "Get your work done, one inadequate sentence and paragraph at a time. Then go through your draft and take out all the lies and boring parts."

BULLETIN

Think of the worship bulletin as signage. What is it communicating about your congregation? Does it match your mission field in terms of sophistication, grammar, taste? Does it have insider language? Does it have good art, not canned clip art, stock images? Is it too thick—or too thin? Does it explain clearly (but not in too many piled-up words) *how* to worship, for the brand-new newbie? Vet your bulletin through a friend who is not a churchgoer, and make the appropriate changes. You can see a copy of our bulletin in the Appendix.

BLESSING EVERYTHING

We bless everything and everyone in our worship. We bless people moving away, new members joining, newly-marrieds, backpacks for the start of the school year, bikes, block-party bouncy houses outside our windows. We develop formal liturgies or just wing it. We try to send the message that everything and everyone can and should be blessed, and we have the power to do it—all of us.

A good little book about with great blessing prayers is Quinn Caldwell's "Bless," available from the United Church of Christ at uccresources.org.

And one of my favorite poems is Marge Piercy's "The Art of Blessing the Day." Here are the last stanzas:

But the discipline of blessings is to taste
each moment, the bitter, the sour, the sweet
and the salty, and be glad for what does not
hurt. The art is in compressing attention
to each little and big blossom of the tree
of life, to let the tongue sing each fruit,
its savor, its aroma and its use.

Attention is love, what we must give
children, mothers, fathers, pets,
our friends, the news, the woes of others.
What we want to change we curse and then
pick up a tool. Bless whatever you can
with eyes and hands and tongue. If you
can't bless it, get ready to make it new.*

ALTERNATIVE WORSHIP

We have done a *lot* of alternative worship. It has all been a gas, but none of it ever blew up into something big and lasting. Maybe we did something wrong, didn't sell it hard enough outside the church, didn't invest the necessary money or people-hours into it. Or maybe, it just was what it was: worship that flowered for a day or a year, and fed some people, and died down to the ground. Some of what we have done:

Rest and Bread: A "commuter communion" service, 45 minutes long, on Wednesday evenings: simple communion, scripture message with a little riff, Taize or other simple songs without sheet music.

Re/New: Dramatic "emergent" style worship in the round, with a big dais of candles at different levels, couches, cushions on the floor. Great music (guitar, piano, percussion), lay preaching, multisensory

*Excerpted from "The Art of Blessing the Day," from *The Art of Blessing the Day*, by Marge Piercy. Copyright 1999 by Marge Piercy. Excerpted by permission of Alfred A. Knopf, a division of Random House, Inc. All rights reserved.

experiences, art supplies, invitation to "choice time" as a response to the sacred text (journaling, artmaking, conversation, walking prayer, etc.).

Advent, Lent and Everyday Morning prayer: A short service (20 minutes) every weekday during Advent and Lent, and Thursdays only during the rest of the year, based on Episcopal morning prayer service. Lay-led, with Christmas lights/low light, no musical accompaniment.

Savor: Savor is a small group supper club for people who are interested in sharing their lives and their stories together while they seek out the life and the story of Jesus. Savor is quite simply a time to gather, to eat and drink, and to talk. In addition, Savor also has a meaningful but easy-going ritual built into it that will help the group to intentionally bring their souls to the table and to discuss the life and teachings of Jesus in relationship to their own lives and experiences. Savor is not really something new. Jesus asked us to remember him at the table. And the earliest Christians, before the gospels were written down, gathered together at festive meals to eat, drink, socialize, and tell stories in memory of Jesus.

SPECIAL WORSHIP

Blue Christmas/Longest Night service: With other area churches and faith communities, a service for the shadow side of the season—especially for those experiencing trauma, grief or depression.

Palm Sunday Donkey Walk: Live donkey with 12-year-old Jesus of any gender, marching and chanting 60s civil rights chants all the way to the village square, where we pray for our city.

Maundy Thursday Last Supper: A table set at the front of the sanctuary, with a Mediterranean feast: pomegranate juice, wine, grape leaves, pita, hummus, feta, olives, clementines. All those gathered feast, then pile up the remains. Twelve take their place behind the table and read scenes from the last twelve moments in the life of Jesus, extinguishing a candle each time. Between the readings, a modern poem as a mirror to the scripture text, and haunting hymns.

Holy Saturday Labyrinth Walk: We draw a chalk labyrinth in our parish hall, keep the lights low, put an ostrich egg dyed red at the center of labyrinth and icons all around, and walk it prayerfully, as the women friends of Jesus walking to the tomb to prepare the body.

"DIFFICULT" PEOPLE IN WORSHIP

In a church that looks like the Kingdom of Heaven, you will not only have queer people and people of every color and economic group worshipping, you will have babies crying, toddlers dancing in the aisle, addicts recovered and otherwise. You will have mentally ill people somewhat dangerously lighting candles, Down's adults praying aloud for every person they can think of, and, my favorite, the congenitally talkative Announcer-type.

We have spent more words than I care to remember, at Deacons and Council meetings, mediating conversation between people who disagreed about proper behavior in worship. Interestingly, in our church, the old and young folk don't really fight about worship. The arguments have often broken down along the lines of newbie/veteran (i.e. pitching worship to beginners versus experienced Christians) and parents/non-parents (i.e., noise tolerance levels in worship).

We do the best we can to balance people's sometimes very varying worship "needs," always mindful of the *75% rule* coined by Rev. James Forbes of Riverside Church: that in a truly vital church, you're only happy with what's going on about 75% of the time, because you're giving up the other 25% for someone down the pew who is different from you, who really needs what you eschew.

A word about mentally ill folk: we have had the psychiatrists/psychologists/social workers in our congregation train our deacons and worship leaders in how to support mentally ill people in worship, especially people who might be acting out in inappropriate or unsafe ways: the aforementioned candle-lighting and wandering around with lit flames, drunkenness, shouting, inappropriate intimate touching/hitting on other members.

We have adopted a phrase from a sister church: all people are welcome, but not all behaviors are welcome. We also operate under a principle that if the hairs on the back of your neck are going up, trust them—don't let being "nice" trump awareness of potential trouble. Jesus said we should be wise as serpents and innocents as doves. The most loving thing we can do with people who are behaving inappropriately is set healthy boundaries for them.

A word about kids in worship: it's complicated. Even in a congregation that loves and welcomes normal levels of kid noise, periodically a parent will appear who seems oblivious to their children's volume or destructive tendency, or worse, thinks it's cute. Someone may need to have a *very* gentle conversation with them, or offer them books/quiet toys/crayons and paper, or even offer to help redirect their child or take them out so the parent can themselves have a quiet hour of worship! Start the conversation from a place of love, not judgment.

And remember: children are not just our future, they are our present. If we send the message that our children are not welcome *as children* and not little adults in our worship services, we'll get exactly what we deserve.

LENGTH OF WORSHIP AND TRANSITIONS

Our worship runs long for mainline Protestants: never less than an hour, usually about an hour 10, sometimes an hour and a half. Nobody ever complains (except for my husband), because (usually) we are good with transitions, it doesn't bog down, and whatever we're doing is nourishing, so people understand the need for it. We sing *a lot* in worship. We pray for a long time, accompanied by music. We bless everything. This takes a while, but we try to be careful not to let one person's voice dominate. It's not the Molly Show, or anyone else's—John Bell says that the worship leaders are not the performers and the congregation the audience; he says that we are all the performers and God is the audience.

Transitions are important. Too little time and our spirits and emotions feel rushed, there's no time for an echo. Too much, and it drags. We gathered a Creative Worship Team and spent about a year evaluating how our worship worked and how to do things so that worship flowed smoothly, made sense, felt transporting, reflected the cultural diversity we longed to embody, honored the children in our midst, and made logistical sense.

MUSIC: BEYOND THE WORSHIP WARS

We don't subscribe to the worship wars at our church—contemporary versus traditional, this hymnal versus that hymnal versus a projector and screen. We have all kinds of music in our worship services. We believe, like the phrase apocryphally attributed to Duke Ellington, that there are only two kinds of music: good music and bad music.

We have had gifted music directors who doggedly sought out great music for worship—attending workshops and connecting with other likeminded worship directors to find the most moving worship music from all over the world. We sing songs that uphold good theology or adapt lyrics to fit our culture (inclusive language, not a once-and-for-all or individualistic idea of salvation, etc). We sing and play classical, gospel, Taize, 70s folk, hip-hop, jazz, Christian camp songs, pop music.

We have danced to ABBA in the round. We have played Crocodile Rock on podcast at the funeral reception of an octogenarian. We have shaken our shimmies to Shakira as a benediction. We have done a mashup of the Hallelujah Chorus and a Russian folk song, or teared up as our children stumble their way through the Black Eyed Peas' "Where Is The Love?" We have wept our way through "O Sacred Head Now Wounded" with cello and clarinet, and sung "O Holy Night" in unison at the top of our lungs, without irony, even if we couldn't quite hit the high notes. The Spirit will not be bound by our tiny distinctions of what constitutes "appropriate" church music.

A SPIRIT OF PERMISSION TO PRAISE GOD, NOT PERFORM

We have lucked into some a-ma-zing professional musicians in our congregation over the years. My personal favorite is when the saxophone player from the 90s band Morphine came to play at a baptism. I may or may not have acted a little starstruck. We have a hip-hop/funk frontliner and a respected Christian folk singer/songwriter, as well as several composers in the congregation.

But the thing I love best about our music program is the lack of pretention and ego, no matter who is playing. What we do in worship is praise God, not perform, and so we let pretty much anybody, with the proper support and direction, play and sing in worship.

Our choir is all-volunteer. We've had all manner of people dust off instruments they haven't touched since junior high or high school—and because of that, not only have they discovered their art anew in the context of offering their spiritual gift (and not in a way that enslaves them to ego), we get *for free* orchestras at Easter, soul bands for Gospel Palm Sunday cantatas, guitar orchestras for the outdoor Blessing of the Animals or Easter Sunrise service, bluegrass bands for Christmas Eve.

MARCHING BAND

You don't know this, but you need a marching band. We started a marching band about five years ago, on a whim, and once we had it, we used it all the time. They guide our feet in parades, like the Honk!fest parade that is a big deal in our neighborhood, and the extravaganza Boston Pride Parade, a big outreach venue for us. They inaugurate our block party and accompany our Palm Sunday Donkey Walk. All you need for a marching band is a solid lead percussionist, a spirit of whimsy and several other musicians of varying talent and instrument. We have had saxophonists, washboard and spoon players, accordion, trombone, 6-foot-something baton twirlers, and more. It *always* works, and introduces a spirit of joy and hilarity.

CHAPTER TEN

Leadership

• • •

Michael Piazza, if you don't know him (and you should!) was the Dean of Cathedral of Hope in Dallas, Texas. If you ever get a chance to hear him speak about anything, *do,* because you will learn a lot.

One thing I learned from Michael was that an organization can only grow as big as the capacity of its leader(s). People can only handle about 60 or 70 "real" relationships; even a workaholic extrovert can't do much more than that. So, when your church passes this mark, you have to figure out how to multiply leadership, or you will naturally stop growing.

Understanding this reality to be true doesn't mean it's easy to do. It's one of the things that comes hardest to me. In some ways I am much better suited to be the solo pastor of a smaller church—that's where I am at ease and know intuitively what to do—I can have a personal relationship with everybody, know what's going on, have a good grip on every relationship, twist and turn, ministry detail.

But that's not the church God gave me, so I needed to develop different skills. Skills of hiring and training good staff, skills of developing lay leadership and delegating responsibility, skills of diffusing responsibility and holding people accountable while not micromanaging. Carey Nieuwof has a few must-read blog posts that distill down to perfection that challenge of leadership, vision and strategy in a growing church.

Here are some of the things we have done to develop our leaders and leadership skills and to keep up with embodying the next size church we have become.

LEADERSHIP NIGHT

About three weeks after our annual meeting, which is when we vote in a new leadership slate, we hold a Leadership Dinner to which we invite every officer and committee member, about 65 people.

At Leadership Night:

- We feed people a good home-cooked meal.
- We orient them to each other and their work so they feel the power of all those different people in all the tasks necessary to making a church our size viable.
- We talk clearly about expectations of our leaders and teams.
- We worship and sing.
- We give them a takeaway on leadership: we've used the Leadership Compass, talked about Rabbi Edwin Friedman and self-differentiation, and this year we'll use John Kotter's 8 principles of leading through change.
- We let them, for the last 15 minutes, move into their committees and teams to bond with each other and begin their work.

At Leadership Night, our people get inspired to work excellently for the whole; they get real wisdom that they can apply not only to church leadership but to the way they do their work and relationships in the rest of their lives. It's meaty and meaningful.

SOCIALIZING BIG DECISIONS

One thing I learned the hard way at the church I used to serve was that if you are going to make a big change, it doesn't need to take years to effect, but it does help to socialize the idea well before the start date. Think out loud, ask for feedback, and let other people's feedback make your big idea better.

Talk about big new ideas a *lot*—not as your idea, but as the church's idea. Let it be a grassroots campaign. Use all the formats at your disposal to communicate—sermon, listserv, newsletter, meetings and meeting minutes, one on one conversations. John Kotter says most leaders under-communicate by a factor of 10. Think about that! Imagine that your last big idea that fell flat, did so not because it was a bad idea but because you didn't talk about it clearly or often enough!

Think about your church's polity and how it governs itself, and get concentric circles of buy-in at the right rate. For example, I am coming up on five years since my last sabbatical. My contract says I get a sabbatical every five to seven years. I had a year of medical leave in the middle of that time, during which I was still doing a little bit of work for the church, but not getting paid or being officially "on." I am ready for my next sabbatical! But it's a little early.

To draw off potential criticism, I got wide buy-in. First I asked my clergy colleague: was he up for me taking a half-sabbatical at five years, and another one at seven years? He said an enthusiastic yes. Next, I got support from my ministerial care team. Of course they said *yes!* Then I could go to the Deacons and say, well, my colleague and Care Team support me. Deacons were also enthusiastic. Next I went to Church Council, and said: everybody's on board with this. So are we! they said. Finally, it will go to the congregation. They'll trust the decision because I introduced it at the right pace, to the right folks.

TRADING UP LEADERS

I went to the National Church Leadership Institute put on by the Center for Progressive Renewal some years ago, a three-day conference for new and renewing church leaders, that covers everything from stewardship to marketing, et alia. At the time, our church was growing but one of our recurring struggles was that some leaders were really strong and motivated, and others were, well. No-shows, or passive-aggressive, or downright toxic. I asked Michael Piazza, who was keynoting there: how did he do it at his gazillion-member church? How did he make it look so easy?

He said: you start where you are, and you just keep trading up. As new people come, you discern people's gifts, try to get them into the right role, and pry ill-equipped people from the wrong roles. Eventually, you get there.

This has turned out to be true—as we have grown, our leadership has grown more mature and secure. Which is not to say it will ever be 100%, and I've come to the conclusion, from looking at the shiny happy outside of lots of fast-growing churches, that it is probably no better over there where the grass looks greener.They're just better at hiding the dirt.

THE J'S HAVE IT

Myers-Briggs is the personality typing test that can tell us a lot about our gifts and capacity, the way we take in information, steward our energy, see the world—and bring projects to completion (or not).

Most pastors, I've heard it said, are Myers-Briggs INFJ's* or ENFJ's. A few are P's instead of J's—dreamers instead of doers. Let me be clear, I'm not privileging one over the other. But you need J's in your church to get stuff finished. P's are great evaluators, which we also need so we're not just doing things willy-nilly, but too many half-finished projects and half-begun programs lying around the church enervates everybody.

*Myers-Briggs is a personality type indicator that defines certain hard-wired characteristics like extroversion and introversion, and "perception" versus "judging." These terms don't necessarily mean what you think they mean. You can do more reading on your own to learn about each type and its strengths.

When we interview people, especially pastor-types, everybody loves to say they're a creative, a visionary. We hardly ever hire those people unless they *also* say they are good at getting stuff done. Because the fact of the matter is, dreaming alone doesn't move the vision along.

Consider having your folks in leadership—or folks you'd like to be in leadership—take a Myers-Briggs test. It will help you understand what their gifts and strengths are so you can put them into the right roles and not doom them—or yourself—to failure.

DIY

As you rebuild/remake/renew, you are going to need some new stuff. And here's the thing about paying for stuff: it adds up. And unless you have a huge endowment (which is a whole different problem—having too big an endowment can be as big an impediment to renewal as having no money at all to play with), it is hard to pay for a lot of new stuff.

Capitalize on the DIY shift that has taken culture by storm. Don't underestimate how powerful an experience it is for people to fix things and build things themselves, even if it takes a little longer. Then, every time they see the work of their hands, they will feel invested in this enterprise of the community, not to mention the friendships and in-jokes and good feeling that are fostered when people give up their free time to make things beautiful and functional.

The best DIY projects don't just utilize people with know-how, but people who know how to cheerlead effectively, to bring a project home. Just as important as having parishioners who know how to sheetrock is having some who know how to send reminders with uncanny timing, write succinct and inspiring emails, collate RSVPs, connect the right people to the right roles, create a sense of fun during the projects and celebrate every victory, however small, sometimes multiple times. You also need people who know how to delegate, and how to teach!

We've done all kinds of things without paid professionals (or with a few paid professionals alongside many unpaid amateurs): ripped up the old carpet in our sanctuary, renovated our chapel to create a new nursery (if you build it, they will come) and a spiritual reading library (we live in a very bookish neighborhood), built tons of IKEA furniture, painted murals in our children's areas, made bean bag chairs from scratch, tore up our front lawn to create a terraced vegetable garden (we invite our neighbors to harvest from it for their own needs, and use the remainder on the coffee hour table/donations to the local food pantry).

DIY projects definitely take more coordination from leadership than calling professionals but they are far less expensive. They also "show-not-tell" the message that this church belongs to all of us, and we are all stakeholders in its destiny.

YOUNG ADULT LEADERS

The average age in our church is about 31. Our last moderator, the senior lay position, was 25 years old when he took the job. Our deacons range in age from 26 to 48. A friend asked me, How do you get young adults to lead? I said: we ask them. It's pretty much that simple.

However: we don't ask them and then tell them what to do, expecting them to be the puppets of the old guard. We don't ask them and then ignore or put down their ideas. We don't ask them then countermand everything they say.

Ask them, then support them—orient them to their roles, make sure they know what their responsibilities and your expectations are, make sure they have the stuff (logins, passwords, money, keys, helpers) they need, and don't expect them to be around forever. Be clear about the length of the term of leadership, and ask them to re-up if you want them back, don't assume they will continue until they burn out (the old model of church leadership). Give them good training that they can apply to other areas of their life, so they see this service as something that feeds their whole vocation!

MISSION STATEMENTS, VISION STATEMENTS, AND BYLAWS

I think the process of wordsmithing a mission statement or a vision statement can be a distraction from the work of leaning into the actual vision. But, you have to start somewhere. We rewrote our mission statement, and wrote a five-year vision statement, for the first time about five years ago (hmm . . .). They're below.

It was a very generative, exciting process, which I wasn't expecting. There were also some fights, primarily over language, primarily over whether we were making the Republicans and Libertarians in the church invisible by calling ourselves theologically progressive (we wanted very badly to distinguish ourselves from the Religious Right, since we live in a very educated, religiously skeptical and even hostile-to-religion area of the country). Almost everybody was happy with the result, and we all learned to live with it.

We have used our statements a lot—not just on the church website, but at every Council meeting and many other important church meetings, to stay focused on our goals and our strategy.

We've also undertaken to update our bylaws, which we have been more or less ignoring for a decade. The conversation around whether the bylaws should be changed to reflect what we currently do, or the kind of church we want to become (which is an even more radical thing), engendered some interesting disagreements. They rather took me by surprise. We are currently a super-low-conflict church, and I thought the bylaws revision would be no big deal. But bylaws still represent the source of power, authority, position, direction and vision of our churches. Why wouldn't there be the potential for a fight embedded in there?

Mission Statement

First Church Somerville UCC is a community of curious and creative spiritual seekers, committed to learning and embodying a progressive practice of Christianity. We walk in the Way of Jesus, striving to love kindness and do justice for all people. We are of many minds in our spiritual beliefs, but one body in loving service to others and in joyful worship of the One who made us.

Vision Statement

First Church Somerville UCC will be a warm, welcoming and diverse church. With prayer and scripture as our foundation, we will provide multiple opportunities to grow deeper in our relationship with God and Jesus Christ, through worship, education, fellowship and justice work. Our church will be clean, bright, environmentally responsible and fully functional for our church members, our children, and the greater Somerville community. We will have increased membership, stable financials and appropriate staffing with the ability to provide staff with health and wellness benefits.

SPIRITUAL GIFTS INVENTORY

We invented the spiritual gifts inventory to flag for us what people really loved to do, the interests and skills that nourish their souls and might also strengthen our community. We rely on this heavily when it's time to think about who to bring into new leadership rotation. There's a link to a Google form version of it in our weekly e-newsletter, and from time to time we will flag it for new people so they know to fill it out.

PLANNING THE FUTURE, NOT REHEARSING THE PAST

One of the best and simplest ideas for helping our congregation look forward, always forward, came from our 27-year-old moderator. We've all been at a Church Council (a.k.a. Vestry, a.k.a. Your Main Group of Players) that went on for hours, during which nineteen committee chairs each rehearsed their last committee meeting in fine detail. At the end of this highlights reel, everybody is bored out of their minds, exhausted, and low-blood-sugar. There is no time to look forward.

Our moderator recast the agenda for our church council meeting. It looks like this:

Opening Devotion (20 minutes)

Where we've been (5-10 minutes)

Where we are (15 minutes)

Where God is leading us (30 minutes)

Closing prayer (5 minutes)

Important Dates Coming up

Our devotional time is intentionally the longest portion of our meeting (well, unless it's budget season!).

Under the "Where we've been, Where we are, and Where God is leading us" sections, we might have one or two projects each to discuss. These are projects that affect the whole church in some capacity: the scope of a building renovation, progress on the new bylaws, the draft budget for the new year, building a covenant with a new mission and justice agency. Each person present at the meeting listens and speaks not for themselves but representing the ministry they are charged with supporting, and the whole of the church—so we see every new project and decision from multiple angles and constituencies.

No committee, at any time during the Council meeting, makes a general report on its activity. As we transitioned to this model, committees that felt they *had* to share what was going on in their committee did, but for no more than two minutes each.

Committees are, of course, welcome to get on the agenda if they have an issue they need broader input on. Our church council holds a lot of credibility, so individual committees will often ask the council to help discern big changes or decisions. We know if we have consensus in council, we will have it throughout the church.

That said, council members also deeply trust their committee chairs and committees to set their own priorities and make their own decisions—we don't spend, say, an hour deciding whether plastic Easter eggs are too environmentally unsustainable for the Sunday school Easter egg hunt. We run efficiently, trust our partners, and let decisions and discussion find the appropriate level.

The result of moving to this type of agenda is shorter meetings (hallelujah!), more energy and excitement, and a whole lot more forward movement.

WHY WE DO WHAT WE DO, AND SPIRITUAL EXHAUSTION

As much as we might wish people would lean into the ego-snuffing Jesus-teaching that says "don't let the left hand know what the right hand is doing . . . when you pray, pray in secret," people need to know their service to their church and God's wider community makes a difference.

I take every opportunity, and encourage other leaders in our church to do the same, to reflect back to people the difference their service and leadership are making. For example, I preached about a woman with end-stage brain cancer, peripheral to our community, to whom just coming to worship made all the difference in her ability to make peace with her death. I called out the people who fold bulletins, who greet at the door, who run the sound booth, all as instruments of God in that woman's journey to peace, acceptance, and across the barrier of death. I tell redemption stories a lot about people in the church, so everyone can see the difference even our little contributions make to the whole.

When we get spiritually exhausted, burn out, lose our faith or our vocation, it's because we've become disconnected from the truth that our service in the community of Christ really matters and makes a difference in the lives of suffering people or a suffering Creation. When we have people who can connect the dots for us, it renews our commitment and our energy.

LEADER FATIGUE

Because rebuilding a church is such an uphill battle, and requires a lot of work, the congregation will have to calibrate its energies. The pastor(s) and lay leaders will learn to intuit when it's time to apply gas to a particular project or direction, and when it's time to coast. I don't say "brake," because braking is a waste of energy. Just as when you drive a car, you waste fuel when you go too fast and then have to brake when you reach a light, good leaders pay attention to the road signs and other visual indicators and try to optimize fuel efficiency.

Certain times of year (summer! Advent! Lent!) are sabbathy times when our focus turns in to our spirits or out toward the body and play. These are not good times to, say, launch a website or undergo a visioning process. Good leaders pay close attention to their people's energy and anticipate or forestall burnout.

Leader burnout can come as a result of working too hard, of working against obstacles, or from doing work that rightfully belongs to someone else. The antidote to leaders working too hard is: helping the leader boundary their work, giving them a longer timeline, or finding them the right partner. The antidote to working against obstacles is: helping remove those obstacles (Do they need space? Money? Direction? Permission? Information?). The antidote to doing work that belongs to someone else is: speaking to the someone else and making sure they understand what is expected of them, and if they can't commit, finding a new someone else, or letting that particular function lie fallow for a while.

One consistent regret I have is when leaders in my church take on too much, fail to fulfill their commitment, and then disappear from church out of guilt or embarrassment. We talk a lot about engagement in our church as vocation—where their deep gladness meets the world's/the church's deep need (a la Fred Buechner)—and that while there are lots of things in the church that need to get done, God doesn't want them to be miserable doing them, or lose their faith community if they feel that they have let us down. We also talk about how Jesus urged us to let our yes be yes and our no be no—to have a clear sense of our own capacity and calling to do particular tasks, and to exercise our "no" regularly as a mark of spiritual maturity.

CHURCH SIZE AND LEADERSHIP

Pastors: you will do radically different things when you pastor your church of 150 or 300 in worship than you did when it was 30 in worship! Note: there will be some loss of cabin pressure, a.k.a. pastoral authority, when you begin to become a program size church and outgrow family size/pastor size church. You may get more pushback. You may feel people don't automatically trust your decision-making as they used to. Do not be alarmed! This is a function of church size and complexity and is to be expected. But it still kind of sucks.

Our growth has plateaued a few times in my tenure. Sometimes, it was seasonal, or related to things we couldn't control, like my cancer diagnosis. Other times, it was directly a result of my leadership capacity being too stretched, and other forces in the church, especially the anxiety around change that would lead people to subconsciously self-sabotage to keep the church cozy and small.

I've mentioned Carey Nieuwof's excellent blog posts on the subject of tensions and stuckness in church size. Don't miss them!

CHAPTER ELEVEN

Church Conflict

• • •

First, go watch a short video on YouTube called "Friedman's Theory of Differentiated Leadership Made Simple."

Now we can talk.

I talked earlier about difficult people in the church. But please don't live in the illusion that if all the difficult people left the church, it would be unicorns and rainbows.

Humans are humans wherever you go, and blaming individuals for church conflict (even though some of them are very strong vectors for it) misses the point that it's not really the individuals, but the anxiety in the system, that allows conflict to take root and do harm. Deal with the anxiety, and you defuse the conflict. The individuals are just the "identified patients," people who are bearing the symptoms of more widely held anxiety.

Radical self-differentiation is the key to defusing anxiety. That, and laughter. Radical self-differentiation, in the words of Edwin Friedman, is "the willingness to take responsibility for your own emotional well-being and destiny." It is the love named in I Corinthians 13 that doesn't insist on its own way, is not irritable or resentful, does not rejoice in wrongdoing, but rejoices in the truth.

Self-differentiation knows where I end and You begin; it uses I statements, it follows the James Forbes 75% rule; it doesn't have secret conversations or use emotional triangles to try to increase power or relieve pressure; it knows how to communicate directly, face-to-face, instead of by email, petition, other indirect and ineffectual means.

Self-differentiation knows how to laugh, even in a difficult situation, and how to use humor to turn things around and reverse the polarity when anxious people are using brinkmanship tactics.

There will always be conflict in the church. Or, rather, in a healthy church there will always be a certain amount of disagreement. Like Fred Buechner's definition of doubt, healthy disagreement in a church is "the ants in the pants of faith. It keeps it alive and moving."

UNHEALTHY PEOPLE

There will always be unhealthy people in your congregation. A friend of mine once said that in a vital ministry environment, 20% of people support your leadership unequivocally, 20% are against you, and 60% are going along with it. I found this a very depressing breakdown! I prefer to work in an environment where I have more support and fewer criticisms. Probably you do, too.

That said, if every single person is on board with your vision, it probably isn't very visionary. Not that you're not an amazing bridgebuilder, but visionary leadership is unsettling. It should even have you a little off-kilter, feeling like you're going over the falls in a barrel.

That said, in even the most harmonious setting, there are a few people who are chronically unhappy and even toxic. There are a couple different kinds of negative people. There are the garden-variety curmudgeons, and then there are the clergy killers and the toxic projectors.

Curmudgeons can be loveable and often are. Even if they don't get their way, and grouse about not getting it, they won't threaten to leave, abuse their power or withhold their pledge. They can be tiring but they don't pose a real threat to the progress and renewal of the church. They can even be won over, with the proper leadership.

Clergy killers are those who go after their settled pastor in a targeted way. They may begin as the pastor's biggest champion, and when the pastor refuses to meet every one of their needs or challenges them directly or indirectly, they turn on the pastor, enlisting others if they can, and push the pastor out, if possible. A female clergy colleague of mine once noted that all the clergy killers she had encountered, the people most resistant to her ministry, were themselves women who had in some sense "failed" in ministry. They once discerned a call to ministry but never entered the process, dropped out of their vocation, or were doing poorly in a similar type of career.

Finally, the "toxic projectors" are unhealthy people who are unwilling or unable to face the pain or chaos in their personal lives, and so distract themselves by choosing an issue or a person (usually the pastor) at the church as their *bête noire.* In healthy churches, their toxicity won't gain much of a toehold and, led in love by healthier leaders, they will either begin to communicate and behave in healthier ways, or they will leave.

It is OK for them to leave! We need to send this message to our healthier, more mature people, so they don't feel guilty when it happens, like they have personally failed. When toxic people who refuse to change their ways stall or kill the renewal of the church, they have killed it for everybody—including the dozens or hundreds of people not yet there who may have benefited from a church like yours.

A friend of mine says, "all people are welcome to our church, but not all behaviors are welcome." It's up to us as pastoral leaders to establish behavioral covenants and norms so that the entire congregation, especially the spiritual leaders (moderator, deacons, pastors, or the equivalent in your setting) can model and reinforce these norms. The norms are things like: speaking for yourself and not on behalf of others, using "I" statements, not making anonymous criticisms or triangulating others into conflict (and not allowing yourself to be triangulated in), not having parking lot conversations about contentious issues with one's allies after the meeting but addressing them in the appropriate leadership setting, with clarity and honesty. See the section on Getting on the Train.

A word about folks with chronic mental health issues: any good church worth its salt *will* have mentally ill people. These people need love and spiritual shelter. In a spiritually healthy environment, they will feel welcomed and learn to be their best selves in community. However, I have had particular difficulty pastoring one particular kind of sufferer with mental illness: folks with borderline personality disorder.

I've had the blessing and curse, over the years, of pastoring several people I suspected of suffering from borderline personality disorder. This disorder is especially pernicious because it often remains undiagnosed, and, even when it is diagnosed, the person who suffers from it remains unwilling or unable to accept their diagnosis.

Unlike a depressed person, who usually understands that they are ill and is grateful for support around their illness, someone with BPD often engages in an all-or-nothing, love-hate relationship with their pastor. They may seem like a "too good to be true" member at the beginning—working hard for the church, professing their great love for the church and for your leadership in particular. But when you do something to let them down, they will turn on you.

I've done some reading and talking to professionals about how to handle folks with BPD. It comes down to being gentle, being loving, being consistent, having clear boundaries, giving specific feedback, and remaining self-differentiated and calm even if the person starts getting personal or going on the attack.

I have kept a journal/written a verbatim of conversations with people exhibiting these behaviors so I can reflect clearly on them later, and have a reliable record to share with other church leaders if that becomes necessary, i.e. if the person makes unfounded accusations or twists my words.

In my experience, some of these folks have cycled out (left the church) and some have cycled through (and later thanked me for helping them, or just ignored the conflict after it was done flaring). All of them have worn me out!

GETTING ON THE TRAIN

We got a most helpful metaphor from one of our church growth consultants, Jim Griffiths, back in the beginning. It has served us really well when things got hot and people got angry and threatened to leave the church because they were not getting their way.

He asked our people, "What if everybody gets on a train in Chicago and the train is going to Boston. But halfway there, somebody says, 'I thought this train was going to Miami! I want to go to Miami.' What do you do?"

Being kind, helpful Christianish people, they said things like, "We could go to Miami first, *then* go to Boston." "We could go back to Chicago, and wait with them until a train to Miami comes along." "We could explain how awesome Boston is." "Why don't we just go to Miami? It's warmer, anyhow."

Our consultant was kind of a hard-nosed character (which is probably why he was a consultant and no longer a church pastor), and he said, "But you decided you want to go to Boston. Are you really going to let one or two people turn a whole trainload of others around?"

We got it. And so, over the years, when someone has said, metaphorically speaking, "I thought our church was going to Miami," and insisted on Miami even after we did explain how awesome Boston is, we have very lovingly let them off the train, and occasionally even pointed out the train to Miami.

The Miami-bound may not have always *felt* it was loving, because they thought the loving thing to do would be to take them where *they* wanted to go. But, and this is boilerplate self-differentiation: the loving thing to do is to encourage them to take responsibility for their own well-being and destiny. And if the pastor and the vast majority of the people have determined that Boston is the destination, well. Keep going to Boston. It's going to take you a while to get there, and going to Miami first is plain foolish, besides not being the journey to which God has called you.

Remember James Forbes' 75% rule: in a truly vibrant, diverse church, any given person is only happy with about 75% of what is going on at any given time. The other 25%, you give up for someone down the pew who really loves it, and needs it, for their soul to be nourished. This applies to hymns, worship style, kid noise levels in church; it applies to new ministries, radical welcome to addicts, homeless folks, mentally ill folks, queer folks and others from the margins; it applies to committee and leadership structures, money and budgeting. The 75% rule applies to any and all issues that have classically divided the church.

AS YOU GROW: PEOPLE WHO DON'T LIKE THE NEXT CHURCH SIZE

So, there is a weird phenomenon in a growing church. The people who bought in when you were one size might not be comfortable growing to the next size. They may try to sabotage the church (consciously or unconsciously) to get it back to the size that is comfortable for them, or they may leave.

If they sabotage it, it's up to you and other healthy leaders to calmly, non-anxiously point out what is going on and help the rest of the congregation to keep the train pointed where you've decided to go.

If they leave, it's sad, but it's appropriate to acknowledge their contributions publicly and bless them on their way. This has happened several times in our congregation, at different stages. We had a lot of introverts at our church—they were happy there because it was a very small church, and easy for them to develop stable, deep relationships. When we began to grow, I suspected the constant influx of new people, and new people who were transient, and new people who took leadership, was very unsettling and exhausting to the introverts. Some of them adapted, and some of them left.

Now that we have a larger church, we attract more extroverts than introverts (but we still think about ways to honor the introverts and help them be comfortable). But some introverts will always be more comfortable in a smaller, more stable-membership church, and they owe it to themselves to find one.

RISK-TAKING AND PERMISSION

We have a lot of big, crazy ideas at our church. We rely on the Holy Spirit to tell us when it's time to act on them, when it's time to wait, and when it's time to dump them. We know when it's time because we have the resources, and the energy, and the right leader(s).

Even then, we widely socialize a new idea for a program or culture-shift. While we are socializing the idea, we say: let's try this for six weeks . . . or six months . . . or a year (whichever makes the most sense for the life-cycle of that idea). We say: we will evaluate after that, and make any necessary changes, or stop doing it. Just that simple act of articulating that every change, ultimately, is temporary, does a lot to lower anxiety and grant permission.

BEHAVIORAL COVENANTS

When things get really out of hand with a disagreement in church—that is, when the rumor mill and the parking lot conversations crank up, factions coalesce, the anonymous complaint box runneth over, anxiety is high and people start behaving badly—a behavioral covenant can get you back on track.

Behavioral covenants give us basic rules of engagement, and remind us how to use non-violent communication even when we want to throttle each other or storm away. Look for a covenant that doesn't use Christian jargon or swirly talk, and that is specific enough in the behaviors it asks us to engage in (or not engage in) that it actually has some teeth.

We were having a hard time recently and used a behavioral covenant to talk through a "case study" of a cultural change we had made a year ago that was still unsettling—the coffee klatch model of coffee hour. The behavioral covenant helped people to speak for themselves, to offer criticism constructively, to listen to understand rather than getting defensive. At the end of the conversation we had a much clearer picture of people's interests, of where the new culture was not working, and some easy, actionable items to improve the model.

For a good example of a behavioral covenant, search online for "Shepherd of the Hills Lutheran Church behavioral covenant."

CHURCH FIGHTS

Our church is very young and has experienced something like 96% turnover in the last ten years—that is, of the almost 300 people currently involved (not counting children), and the 600 people overall who have been connected in some way over the last decade, only about a dozen people have been there longer than ten years.

You would think, given the degree of turnover, that the church fights would have been generational: old vs young. They have not been. Our old people are amazing permission-givers. We have patriarchs and matriarchs who cry at same-sex weddings (with joy); they say "You have to put the young people in charge of things—and then you can't tell them how to do their job."

I don't know what the secret is—they were like that when I got here. I suspect it has something to do with keeping anxiety low, fostering loving relationships between old and young (so much permission derives from love and trust, doesn't it?), and knowing that without the young ones, they would have no church to be buried out of. It's enlightened self-interest.

The frictions we have endured as a church in the last decade have fallen along these lines instead:

- no-kids versus kids in worship
- experienced Christians versus Bible babies/Nones
- passive-aggressive leaders and self-differentiated leaders
- small church people and medium church people (which, to some degree, has manifested as tension between the character of introverts and the character of extroverts)

I won't go into every one of these disagreements. But I will say a few things:

I think we were able to respond to the legitimate desires of both new and more experienced Christians by really developing our liturgy, getting coded language and jargon out, doing more exegesis aloud, and honestly, when the lead preacher (me) began doing more and better homework on the texts as I prepared the sermon, so the text got more rooted deep down into me—not for the purpose of "showing off my learning" but so the sermon wouldn't be shallow and self-helpy. We also run a wide variety of Bible studies throughout the year, for every level.

The small church/medium church tension continues to be a bit of a struggle. Some people who join your church when you are 45 in worship, and who get to know everybody, are just never going to be able to make the transition and will leave when you reach 90 or 100 in worship.

Remember, even in a healthy, well-managed church disagreement, people will probably leave. This is OK! Leaving will allow you to move forward with your vision and allow them to find a new church home that is a better fit. Of course, you want them to leave well—with reasonably good feelings on both sides, clear about what they want in a new home church so they can find one that fits, their real friendships with church members intact. This is entirely possible, with good communication and clarity, behavioral covenants, laughter and trust.

NEWBIES

In our church, people know that newbies come first. This is not because newbies are intrinsically better. It's because they don't have any relationships or power yet. They deserve our kindness and our very best attention for this reason.

It can be downright terrifying to walk into a church for the first time. People are coming with a lot of baggage, and a lot of trauma, spiritual questions or doubts, fearing judgment or worse—fearing being ignored or unseen. For this reason, newbies are the "weaker members of the body" (I Corinthians) to whom we give special attention. We had a young woman come to church last year who wouldn't "permit" herself to come to worship until she had come to a whole bible study series—she felt she didn't have enough security in her spiritual opinions to deserve being in worship! This is just one of the demons people are up against when they walk through the sanctuary doors.

My congregation understands this, acts upon it, and doesn't get mad at their pastors when we wave them away at coffee hour, refusing to transact church business, because to do so means missing opportunities with vulnerable newcomers.

LAUGHTER AND HUMOR

If I needed heavy word count to emphasize the importance of this section, you would be reading a novel by Proust here. But I'll keep it simple.

Laughter is a ministry unto itself. Our church came back from the dead not because we were younger, or hipper, or smarter. We came back from the dead because even when things looked really bleak, even when we disagreed, even when we were talking or preaching about things that were really big and really hard, we always managed to laugh, and we still do.

We take God seriously, but not so much ourselves, or anything else. We have a lot of naturally funny people in the congregation, and that helps. But I actually think we have a lot of naturally funny people in the congregation because there is an atmosphere of lightness and permission-giving around humor and lots of other things.

We cuss sometimes. We tell the truth. And we have a lot of fun. Our humor is not at other people's expense. I wish I could give you an example. But it's like explaining a joke: it wouldn't be funny to you to give you a transcript of, say, our last Church Council meeting. You had to be there.

All's I can say is: if you can manage your own anxiety, and set the tone by being playful, lighthearted, looking for the funny, and outing it, a culture of laughter will take hold. It is infectious—and, as Anne Lamott says, "Laughter is carbonated holiness."

CHAPTER TWELVE

Epic Failures

• • •

When our former moderator (he retired, after seven years, at the grizzled old age of 31) read a draft of this book, he said, "You mention that failures are inevitable—but then you only wrote about our successes!"

The blessing of having a forward-looking constitution like mine is that it is hard to remember our failures. I constantly curate (some would say, rewrite) our history to make it sweeter than it actually was when we were living through it. If I revisited the pain of the past too acutely, I'd lose nerve for the future, and my people along with me.

But for you, gentle reader, I did some dredging. Here are some of our most difficult, dreary, frightening and/or enervating failures along this journey.

The epic plateau of 70 people in worship

Every Sunday morning for many years, I would climb the steps to the chancel, and wonder: how many people will come today? Will enough of them come that we won't feel like losers? And at 9:55 or even 10:02 or 10:10 (we are a tardy crowd), I would hold my breath, and hope and pray, and try not to count.

Because it's not about the numbers. Right?

Except that there are practical considerations. You preach differently to twenty people than you do to forty. And eighty people in worship feels entirely different from forty—much more "critical mass," depending upon the size of your worship space.

Our sanctuary comfortably holds about 250 people, and uncomfortably, about 325. I know that because these days, we are standing-room-only for Easter morning. But when I started out at First Church Somerville, nearly everybody who came could have a huge pew to themselves. It was very demoralizing.

I never let on how demoralizing. I had to fake an enthusiasm and confidence I didn't always feel. I had to make sure that every single individual who came through that door felt like they were *enough,* because the truth is that they *were* enough. They were God's, and so was I, and where two or twenty are gathered in Christ's name, He is there among you.

And because of the sometimes-faked confidence and the genuine love in the room, and because worship was consistently good and real and moving, with tears and laughter, we began to grow. We grew painstakingly: five and ten at a time.

Then we seemed to spend a *long* time with between 60 and 85 people in worship. They were 60 or 85 fantastic people, and I was grateful for every one of them, but I knew it wasn't sustainable: we were still running deficits, and in a high-churn community like Somerville, where we lost 10% of our community a year to Buffalo or San Francisco or Togo, that 10% was deeply felt.

I remember despairing to our church growth coach one time that we seemed "stuck" at that size—which is not unusual. Most people can only manage about 60-85 relationships, and in a small church where intimacy and "knowing everyone and everything" is prized, congregations often unconsciously sabotage further growth.

We knew that getting people into smaller circles—go smaller to get bigger—was the key to breaking the cycle, but we didn't seem to be very good at it. Our wider culture didn't support it: people were busy in their out-of-church lives and found it hard to commit to a weekly or even monthly gathering. (Interestingly, we have had much better luck getting people to commit to doing the work of the church—people for the most part like to feel valued and engaged, and like to have a concrete way to give back when they have discovered a church that feels like home.)

Our church growth coach told me: "Just add the next ten. Then add the next ten. Don't worry about the timeline." That's exactly what we did, and now, I am happy to report, it has been quite a while since I counted heads at 10:10 a.m. Five days, to be exact.

Something kind of magical did happen when we regularly began breaking the 100 barrier in worship—when it became a consistent and not a fluke thing. Big begets big. People began inviting their friends to church in greater numbers—perhaps they finally felt confident themselves in the durability of our community, enough to share it with outsiders. We now average 140 on Sundays, with about 325 people who are on our "currently attending" spreadsheet. It feels great.

And, the small groups are finally working. Maybe it was doggedness, maybe the gifts of our fantastic associate pastor, who is charged with community-building and spiritual formation, or maybe just: patience.

The spontaneously combusting church administrator: For many years, we could not keep a church administrator to save our lives. We couldn't afford to pay for enough hours to make it a viable position, the office was leaky and cold in winter, leaky and stifling in summer. We went through about eight administrators in as many years. Even though some of them moved on to better things, not in spite of but *because* of First Church Somerville—one went to seminary, and one moved out of her role so she could become a church member because she'd become so smitten—it didn't change the fact that we were always seeking, training or saying goodbye to another admin.

I'm happy to report that our current admin has lasted more than two years and is the glue that holds the whole shebang together. I bring her flowers and dainties every day. Actually, I don't, but I ought to—and I make sure she knows just how highly we value her so she will Never Leave.

The spontaneously combusting Buildings and Grounds chair: Like the church admin position, the (unpaid) position of chair of our Buildings and Grounds Team has seen a vicious churn. Some churches are lucky enough to have a skilled young retiree who loves to putter about the church fixing things. In Somerville, where the average age is something just north of toddler, no such luck. All of our B&G chairs have had kids, jobs, aging parents and other things to keep them busy (jerks)—so, though they have, to a one, done their best, none of them has last more than a couple years of being the go-to for cranky boilers, burst pipes, and, coming round again, another All Church Work Day.

You shouldn't play favorites with church leaders, but if you have someone who loves to take care of your building—take care of them.

Sacred Cows and Basketball Trophies: The closest I have come to outright anarchy among my congregation is when, early on, we were giving the room known as the Ladies' Parlor a facelift. It was the most comfortable room in our church: big windows, lots of light, cushy chairs and decent carpeting. However, it needed painting and decluttering, a little feng shui action (anyone who doubts that gay men are a desirable addition to your congregation: just see what magic they can work on the ambiance of a church with $100 and a trip to TJ Maxx).

I made two big boo-boos. First, I boxed up the ancient plastic basketball trophies from the 50s that graced the mantelpiece and put them in a closet. What I didn't know was what the trophies represented: the icon of First Church's glory days, the days of the church basketball leagues and our preeminence among them. The Ladies of the Ladies'

Parlor were irate. I sheepishly unboxed them, and asked my father to build a trophy case for them—but in a hall, not in the Parlor. The Ladies were delighted.

My second mistake was trying to rename the room the People's Parlor, a misguided tribute to the People's Park in Berkeley, California. The Ladies weren't having it. We compromised: since it was now used by people of every gender, it would heretofore be known as: The Parlor. And so it is, to this day.

Severing: Ministers are terrible at firing people, as it turns out. Well, I am, anyhow. My usual MO, when I notice someone is not meeting expectations, is to give a little kind feedback with an earsplitting grin, hoping they "get it." If nothing changes, I do the same thing over again. If still nothing changes, I allow the person in the position to become so completely appalling or ineffectual at their job that it becomes totally obviously to everyone.

And then I say something like, "It's clear to me that you don't really want to be in this position anymore, since you haven't cleaned the bathrooms in eight months." Then, when they act surprised and make a half-hearted show of indignation, I take them and show them the poo streaks and the dust bunnies.

I know that a good supervisor/manager gives clear and timely feedback, throttles up and sets a timeline for improvement if there is no response to the initial feedback, and then severs neatly and according to the proposed timeline for improvement or firing. It's the fair thing to do: to give people an opportunity to step up and change if they can, and to ask them to be responsible for themselves if they don't. I am getting better at this with age and practice (thankfully, not a *lot* of practice), but I'm still not very good at it.

Children's Ministry Starts and Stops: I probably made it sound like: hey, we built a nursery, and poof! babies appeared. In truth, we built our children's ministry program the way we built the numbers in worship: painstakingly, one and two and five children at a time. There were boom times, and times when kids would seem to vanish for no explicable reason.

It is harder to grow Sunday school attendance than it is to grow worship attendance, because of the resources necessary. If your church attendance is wildly inconsistent, it is pretty easy to adapt worship. But if your Sunday school attendance fluctuates a lot, it makes it hard to staff and plan appropriately.

We have always staffed for the next size church we wanted to be, and that has seemed to work. But there's a great desire to want to overpromise to families who are looking for strong religious education programming for their kids.

I still think of one family who came when our church was still pretty small, but clearly well on our way to revitalization. One of the moms owned a very popular local toy store. They had three children. It would have been such a coup for us! I greedily talked them up at coffee hour. They grilled me about programming, youth group, curriculum. "Youth group . . . someday!" I chirped, adding, "And we're, um, sort of between curricula right now. We're sort of between Sunday school teachers too—but our volunteers are *so* nice!"

I could see the light go out of their eyes. Still in denial, I told myself they'd be back—how could we have failed to charm them with our winsome, plucky ways? Besides, there wasn't a single other mainline church in Somerville with a stronger Sunday school than ours! Ours was the best of the worst! But I never saw them again. Those parents knew what they wanted, and it was for the best that we didn't promise them what we couldn't deliver.

Seven years later, we have a youth group. And so many enthusiastic volunteer youth advisors that they outnumber the youth. But, to everything a season.

The Baptism and Bylaws Controversy: The freshest, and therefore most painful, failure relates to our bylaw revision process and our theology of baptism.

In our denomination, each individual church writes its own bylaws. In many UCCs it is common practice to expect that formal members will be baptized. We recognize any Christian baptism—we don't "rebaptize" Catholics or evangelicals. But the fact remains that more and more of the people who find a home at First Church Somerville were raised "nothing," in their words, and therefore were never baptized.

They know they love our church, but they don't feel they know enough about the Bible, Christian history and theology to claim baptism for themselves yet, and so the idea of baptism becomes a stumbling block to entry into the heart of things in our community. Many of them have, in fact, eventually gotten baptized—but after years with us. In the meantime, their friends and spouses and children have all joined the church.

Not that "joining" is the important thing (see "Don't Worry About Joiners"). But, it's a marker of commitment, and belonging. And so the rule about baptism effectively creates a second-class citizen status for those who didn't, in my words, "luck" into an infant baptism. Prevenient baptism becomes a sort of unearned privilege.

When we finally got around to updating our bylaws, which we'd been ignoring for years, our associate pastor and I brought up the baptism issue, and proposed changing it. We met with both intense support and intense opposition: people who understood our theology and approach, and people who felt that the commitment to be baptized was an important marker of faith development and ought to be required for every member, notwithstanding the "unfairness" of those who'd lucked into their baptism at an early age.

We responded creatively, by preaching and talking more publicly about baptism—what it is, why we do it. We do more baptisms: twice a summer, we go on a field trip to nearby Walden Pond (remember Thoreau?) and invite people to renew their baptismal vows by full immersion, and baptize any adults or children who are ready to take that step. Some people feel less threatened getting baptized in a non-churchy setting, and it is also just *fun.* We do all these things to make baptism a "normal" part of our culture, and get even Nones comfortable with the idea.

And, ultimately, we deferred the discussion on whether or not to change that bylaw right now. Even though it is a pain to change our bylaws, requiring a vote of the entire congregation, even I recognized that we were trying to make something happen that wasn't ready to happen.

Just because your congregation is full of young people doesn't mean that, when push comes to shove, things like bylaws don't matter! Even though we ignored them for years, there was still something about the act of re-ratifying them that surfaced hidden power dynamics and internal cultural disagreement.

A LAST (9) WORD(S)

My friend Sue Dickerman, gone to glory, when I was just starting out in ordained ministry said to me: "If you love your people, and they love you, there is nothing you can't do together." It doesn't mean they won't get edgy or upset, but you won't make enemies. They are looking for leadership—give it to them.

ACKNOWLEDGEMENTS

Yours be the glory, Resurrected One. You showed us how it was done, so we would not lose courage or grow faint on the journey.

My eternal thanks to my editor at Pilgrim Press, Tina Villa, for her perspicacity, wit, warmth and permissiveness! I'm so grateful for this opportunity. Thanks to Rev. Maren Tirabassi and Rev. Quinn Caldwell who schooled me in the biz of publishing, to Ann Poston who took a chance on me, to Wendy Vanderhart, Jeff Mansfield and all my UCC colleagues who cheered me along the way—and from whom I've borrowed a lot of great bits. It all belongs to the Holy Spirit, right?

Thanks to early readers Ian, Elizabeth, Jeff, and Jamie—and to my congregation that is so supportive, never once asking, as others might, "Why are you writing instead of taking care of us?" This book is about *your* work—I am merely your muse!

Thanks to the many elders in my church who demonstrated that being old doesn't mean being stuck: you deserve much of the honor for allowing us to take your cherished church in new directions, Dibbie, Barbara, Dick, Virginia, Janet, Agnes, Priscilla, Lois, Roy, Frannie, Edith and many more.

Deep thanks to Stevie McFarland, dear one, cover muse, and blog wrestler.

And finally, to my hilarious, beautiful, generous family: my husband Peter, son Rafael and daughter Carmen, who tolerated my many hours at the computer (get your own lunch, please!) so I could put what our church has learned into the service of others.

Appendix

Resources for Further Learning and Inspiration

This isn't an exhaustive list. An exhaustive list is, well, exhausting. I have read and watched and gone to a *lot* of stuff related to ministry/church growth/worship in the last ten years. These are just a few of the very best things I have given my time to, and recommend you do as well:

BOOKS AND AUDIO

ON STEWARDSHIP

Not Your Parents' Offering Plate, J. Clif Christopher

ON PREACHING/WORSHIP

Preaching, Fred Craddock
Craddock Stories, Fred Craddock
The Art of Pastoring, William C. Martin
13 Ways to End a Sermon, Fred Craddock
A Gift of Improbable Blessing, Maren Tirabassi (for great prayers and creative Bible studies)
To Dance With God, Gertrud Mueller Nelson

ON CHURCH GROWTH

The Big Small Church Book, David R. Ray
The In-Between Church: Navigating Size Transitions in Congregations, Alice Mann

ON CHURCH CONFLICT AND CULTURAL CHANGE

Generation to Generation, Edwin Friedman
A Failure of Nerve, Edwin Friedman
Leading Change, John Kotter
Getting to Yes, Roger Fisher, William L. Ury and Bruce Patton [Harvard Negotiation Project]
Difficult Conversations, Douglas Stone, Bruce Patton, Sheila Heen and Roger Fisher [Harvard Negotiation Project]
How Your Congregation Works, Peter Steinke

EVERYDAY THEOLOGY AND DEVOTIONAL READING

Stitches, Anne Lamott
Help Thanks Wow, Anne Lamott
Travelling Mercies Anne Lamott
Eat This Bread, Sara Miles
An Altar in the World, Barbara Brown Taylor
Pastrix, Nadia Bolz-Weber
Carry On, Warrior, Glennon Melton
Practicing the Way of Jesus, Mark Scandrette
Getting Ready for Baptism, Stillspeaking Writers' Group
I Do! Getting Ready for Marriage: Today's Guide for Couples, Stillspeaking Writers' Group

WEBINARS, COACHES, WORKSHOPS/RETREATS

Center for Progressive Renewal, especially the National Church Leadership Institute

Crossroads Program/New Beginnings

Paul Nickerson, Nickersoncoaching.com

Jim Griffiths, Griffithcoaching.com

Maren Tirabassi's writing workshops

New Members Joining Liturgy

Call new members forward one at a time.

As they come forward, have candles lit, and place them on the communion table.

Invite Senior Deacons forward.

Molly: As I call your name, new members, will you please rise and come forward with a candle representing the light that is in you? We ask you to leave this candle on the communion table as a symbol of your willingness to bring what lights you up into our community, so that you may share it generously with us. Stand, and enter into the heart of all things.

Molly: Church, we want to introduce you to your new siblings in Christ.

Molly: We have some of the usual suspects here: doubting and faithing people raised Catholic, and raised in the UCC, and raised with no religion at all. We have several folks who found refuge as teenagers in fundamentalist churches but couldn't square it with their deep knowledge that God loves gays, just as they are.

Jeff [our associate pastor]: We have several people who as 7-year-olds were already mystics, deeply perceptive but also aware of how fragile and terrifying and beautiful life is.

Molly: We have people who have walked through the valley of the shadow of anxiety and depression, of abusive relationships and long-term unemployment. Here, they have found a peace that is not as the world gives.

Jeff: We have granddaughters who love, love, loved their grandmothers, who learned the truth of life from them: let go and let God.

Molly: We have folks who were once the weird kids, and now know the truth: they are the cool kids.

Jeff: We have two young women who came out of the closet: as former sorority sisters!

Molly: We have an actress, a chaplain, a musician, a librarian, a therapist and a physical therapist, and a concierge.

Jeff: We have our capital campaign consultant, who came to our church to do a job and found a new spiritual home!

Molly: They come from Malden and Worcester, from Ohio and California.

Jeff: We have people who have struggled their whole lives to know they are good enough, and are finally giving up and accepting that they are good and bad, but most of all, beloved, by the God who made them, and now by the folks in here, their church, our church.

MEMBERSHIP PROMISES

Molly: Today we make a covenant, one with another. New members, you make promises to us, before God, so that we know that we can count on you. And we make promises to you, before God, so that you know that you can depend on us through good times and hard times. You have a church and a people. And so now we ask you:

PROMISES FROM THE NEW MEMBERS

Jeff: Do you desire to affirm your baptism into the faith and family of Jesus Christ? If so, please say I do.

I do.

Do you promise to be Christ's disciple, to follow in the way of Jesus, to resist oppression and evil, to show love and justice, and to be a witness to the healing ministry and the loving message of Jesus Christ as best you are able? If so, please say I promise, with the help of God.

I promise, with the help of God.

Molly: Do you promise, according to the grace given you, to grow in your faith, celebrating Christ's presence and furthering Christ's work in all the world? If so, please say I promise, with the help of God.

I promise, with the help of God.

Do you promise to participate in the life and mission of this family of God's people, sharing regularly in the worship of God and enlisting in the work of this local church as it serves this community and the world? If so, please say I promise, with the help of God.

I promise, with the help of God.

PROMISE FROM THE CHURCH

Jeff: Will the members of First Church please rise: Do you promise to help these gathered find their place in the body of Christ, to pray with and for them, to welcome them fully in holy friendship, to be angels for them in times of distress and servants to them in times of need? If so, please answer, We promise, with the help of God.

We promise, with the help of God.

WELCOME

Let us, the members of First Congregational Church, United Church of Christ, express our welcome and affirm our mutual ministry in Christ.

We welcome you with joy in the common life of this church. We promise you our friendship and prayers as we share the hopes and labors of the church of Jesus Christ. By the power of the Holy Spirit may we continue to grow together in God's knowledge and love and be witnesses of a Christ who is alive and well and at work in the world.

You've brought your light to us, we don't leave you empty-handed. We give you a red marble as a symbol of belonging. You are encouraged to keep this marble with you through good times and hard times, and lots of everyday times. Feel your marble in your pocket, and know that you have brothers and sisters praying for you. Come upon your marble in your purse while digging for change, and remember to dig into your hearts to offer prayers for others.

[Deacons hand out marbles and membership certificates, stand shoulder to shoulder with them.]

Blessing: Loving Mother God, give to these your children strength for life's journey, courage in time of suffering, the comfort of faith, love that cannot die, laughter in the company of friends, and the hope of new life; through Jesus Christ, who makes us one. Amen.

Welcomer Training

BACKGROUND: THE STRUCTURE

People decide in the first 4-8 minutes if a church feels safe enough to come back.

Keys to first impression:

- Parking (do we need to put out cones? Have valet parking? Put a sign up about "if you get a parking ticket, leave it in the church office and we'll take care of it"?)
- Signage
- Cleanliness of bathrooms
- Atmosphere when they walk in the church
  - Is there music playing?
  - Smell of coffee/coffee and snacks available?
  - People around and talking?
  - Other ideas?
- Orientation (& disorientation)
  - Greeter on landing
  - Another greeter at entryway to sanctuary
  - Mobile welcomers

If you have a friend coming to church for the first time, ask them to fill out our "Hospitality Checklist."

THE ROLE

Welcomers role:

- Say "are you new?" (don't make assumptions)
- Brief tour—ask if they need:
  - Bathroom
  - Elevator/assistance because of a disability
  - Child care
  - Show them to our nursery space if they have younger kids (0-2 stay in nursery, 3-6 start in nursery but go with Seth and Stacey, there is a new sign-in policy, and tell them about Safe Church!! Two adult rule!)
  - Find out who is teaching older kids and match them up if they have older kids.
  - Give them a copy of our Safe Church brochure

Give them brochure about the church
Ask them if they have any questions about the UCC/our service

- If they are open to it, ask them what their needs are, and what they are looking for in a church, what brought them in today
- If they are alone, offer to sit with them during the worship service; make sure they understand the order of worship (i.e. finding the right hymn in the hymnal)

The Welcomer should be someone who is a little extroverted (by nature or by practice!), someone sensitive who can "read" the newcomers and determine their comfort level and needs

We should be making at least **3 contacts** with a newcomer on the first day: this could be as simple as finding out their name and saying "I'm glad you're here today."

If you didn't sit with them during church, **find them** in the receiving line and wait with them! This is a critical moment!

Ask them to sign the guest book and leave their address!

After church, invite them to coffee hour. If they want to come, ***don't* leave them alone!** Church business can wait until later. This is a socially awkward time even for veterans. Try to introduce them to at least two other people based on their interests.

Follow-up strategy: If newcomers get a face-to-face visit in the first 24 hours, they are 85% more likely to return. Within 48 hours, 60%, and at the end of the week, 15% likely to return. If it's the minister visiting, cut all those percentages in half!!

The minister writes a follow-up note. Dibbie, or Ian and Melissa, deliver a mug to everyone (except those in apartment buildings) within a 2.5 mile radius by Wednesday.

If a visitor comes twice, Liz D makes them a name tag.

Do we have any ideas for a follow-up "gift" for apartment-dwellers?

Any other future projects to work on?

THE ROLE PLAY!

Have everybody practice welcoming, in front of the whole group, in dyads. This is intimidating—and will make the real thing seem easy by comparison!!

Give them some demographics to work with: e.g. the Welcomer plays him/herself, but the newcomer might be:

- A single mom, coming in late, embarrassed and harried
- A fifty-something single man or woman
- A young lesbian or gay couple
- A Tufts undergrad
- Someone with obvious mental health issues, or homeless

What are some of the issues unique to each demographic?

Senior Minister Job Description

(Three-Quarter-Time, 30-35 hours/week)

The Senior Minister is the lead visionary and big-picture advocate for the church. She has primary responsibility for Sunday morning worship, writes most of the outward-facing text promoting the FCS community in our mission field, handles strategic development including communications and public relations, capital campaign and annual stewardship appeal, and goal-setting and vision development for the congregation. The Senior Minister also shares pastoral care responsibilities with the Associate Minister.

Worship: with deacons and Worship Team, oversight over Sunday morning worship and special worship (Holy Week, Lent, Advent). Liturgist and announcer recruitment and training, development of sermon series, and preach 3 times/month.

Public Relations and Communications: with Communications Team and Growth Team, will develop materials for branding/advertising/social networking, write op-ed pieces and blog on behalf of our faith community. Her role is strategic vs. administrative. Will staff outward-facing events as appropriate: mission partner galas, Save Our Homes walk, etc.

Pastoral Care: SP will hold both morning (weekly) and evening (monthly) office hours. SP will be available for 2 weekly pastoral care sessions during the workday, and be available generally by email or phone.

Committee Oversight: SP will serve as an *ex officio* member of all boards and committees. See a list below of the committees for which the Senior Minister has primary responsibility. The Senior Minister will attend no more than 9 evening meetings/month, including standing committees, ad hoc committees, special projects and events outside FCS (wider UCC, wider Somerville) that bespeak a First Church presence.

Funerals/Weddings/Baptisms: The Senior Minister will share responsibility with the AP for these events in the life of the church.

Wider church involvement: The Senior Minister will share responsibility with the AP for meeting with Somerville clergy and planning joint worship events. the Senior Minister will be participate in wider UCC in appropriate balance with local church responsibilities: attending annual Day of Covenant, monthly UCC clergy support group, and occasional other events.

Administration and Supervision: Write the majority of newsletter "pastor's letter" articles, write recommendations for laypeople or former staff, write grants, and staff ad hoc committees such as search committees when appropriate. Supervise church administrator, associate pastor and student minister.

Time off: The Senior Minister will have 6 weeks/year for vacation, up to 1 week/year for professional development, up to 1 week/year for wider UCC participation (General Synod attendance, Silver Lake volunteering). On Sundays when the SP is not preaching, she may exercise the option to participate in worship from the pews.

Narrative / Spiritual Budget

First Church 2010: Walking in the Way of Jesus

"Give, and it will be given to you. A good measure, pressed down, shaken together, running over, will be put into your lap; for the measure you give will be the measure you get back." Luke 6:38

Our Plan for Ministry

2009 is proving to be a life-giving year for First Church Somerville. This year has been a time of providing strong structures to support our recent growth, the better to retain new folks, nourish existing members, and meet spiritual need. We continue to make significant strides in four areas of ministry: worship, spiritual formation, outreach and mission. All are outlined below.

For the last few years, we have been blessed with grant money from several sources. This income allowed us to take risks that have brought us to a place of vitality and sustainable growth, including hiring our Minister of Outreach and developing new programs and initiatives. In 2010, we begin to wean ourselves from these revenue streams, and become fully financially responsible for ourselves as maturing Christians in a faith community they love. We have the means, and I know we can accomplish this. I am asking you to give generously to your church, in the hope and confidence that God will continue to work through First Church Somerville UCC for many years.

To provide life-changing worship every week of the year.

This past year our Sunday morning worship continued to attract even more people. Worship attendance was up from an average of 65 to an average of 85 each Sunday, with a high of 229 people worshipping the God of Resurrection with us on Easter.

We strengthened the midweek service, Rest and Bread, with greater lay participation. Thursday morning prayers continue every week of the year, and expand to daily prayers for Advent and Lent, providing people with a spiritually grounding place to start the day.

We also began the once-a-month worship service re/New for a fresh generation of seekers. In the year ahead, we hope to invest more fully in re/New as an entry point for people who might not otherwise dare to enter the doors of a traditional church, but who deeply desire a relationship with God.

In 2010, our new bells and bell choir will enhance our musical program. We will train and equip a New Fangled Altar Guild to beautify our worship space each week, and we will begin to envision sanctuary renovations that would make our main worship space more sacred, comfortable, environmentally sustainable, and flexible.

Your pledge at work might make way for:

- A lesbian couple who comes with their children. They've been greeted politely but with a little awkwardness at other churches; at one, no one spoke to them at all. Here, they find respect, shelter, family.
- An octogenarian who has seen too many things change in her lifetime and wants this one thing to stay the same: to be buried from the church where she was baptized, after all her friends' churches have closed. She knows her church will be here for her, even if she can't physically attend, and especially when she dies.

- A young adult who visits, hoping he isn't the only person under 40 and isn't mobbed for his youthful energy. He isn't, and he's not. Instead, he finds permission here to do church differently, and he is encouraged to dust off the piece of band equipment he played back in junior high, to play on Easter.

When any of these people miss a Sunday morning, now, they feel like something essential is missing from their lives.

Budget total: $77,520

(Includes a percentage of the pastors' and administrator's salaries; the pastors' utilities, expenses and insurance; worship supplies; music director, organist and musical guests; janitor, music ministry budget; telephone, internet, copier, insurance maintenance and utilities)

To nurture adults and children in their spiritual development, wherever they are on life's journey.

Three of the four staff members hired in 2009 are dedicated to the nurture and spiritual development of our children. Erin Iwanusa underwent formal Godly Play training to build a nurturing, creative Montessori Sunday school classroom and culture for our 3-6 year-olds. Missy, a gifted mentor and Christian leader, teaches the Flying Hedgehogs (our 7-11 year-olds). Renae, a licensed day care provider with 20 years of experience, now provides a consistent presence in the nursery so parents can have an hour of peace and uplift in worship. The children's program, correspondingly, has grown; approximately 40 babies and children now participate.

In the year ahead, we will fully fund all three classroom positions, as well as further training for the teachers and volunteers so that they feel confident and equipped in their roles. We will continue to invest in Godly Play by buying materials we are not able to make ourselves, so that the children can better experience this paradigm-shifting way of imagining Jesus, and children and parents can have a way to enrich their spiritual education at home.

As our church outgrows the capacity for "everyone to know everyone," small groups become an essential part of adult education. They provide a way for people to meet, build relationships, become deeper disciples, receive pastoral care, and grow commitment to the larger body. Molly and Laura Ruth will receive training and will train others in the art of making small groups vital. We will also continue to meet with folks individually for spiritual direction on an ad hoc basis, asking challenging questions to help them get to the next level of faith maturity.

We will continue to support established small groups—New Old Fashioned Bible Study, Rooftop People, Compassionate Caregivers—and other modes of spiritual exploration. Our annual retreat will become two retreats: the winter retreat at Friendly Crossways, and a new fall retreat at Silver Lake Conference Center, our retreat center in western Connecticut. Our congregational book fund will continue to provide study Bibles and other spiritual reading at no cost to those who can't afford them.

Your pledge at work might make way for:

- A twenty-something who comes with questions, even anger, about God. We accept them with all their doubts, and train them to be a liturgist, finding words for their spiritual path. A few years later, we throw a party for their ordination.
- An engaged couple who meets with one of the ministers for premarital counseling. What they learn helps them avoid some big battles with in-laws in their first year of marriage. And God is invited to their wedding.
- A father who did not grow up with religion, but in beginning his own family finds a desire for a spiritual home. He and his infant son are baptized at the same time, amidst tears.

With the help of the church, they find a newfound intimacy with Jesus and enter a richer phase of meaning in their relationships and work lives.

Budget total: $27,360

(Includes a percentage of the pastors' salary; the pastors' utilities, expenses and insurance; the secretary, two Sunday school teachers and a nursery caregiver, budgets for art supplies, books, furniture that needs replacing, training for Godly Play, congregational book fund, telephone, internet, copier, insurance maintenance and utilities)

To reach others who may need a faith community like ours.

This year, we reprised successful outreach and growth efforts: boosting participation at ArtBeat, giving our neighbors a way to meet and mingle at the Block Party. We offered new events, such as Sacred Conversations on Race, which brought many new people to our church for the panel discussion on race and the evening of arts and entertainment.

We welcomed twenty new members, with folks already lining up for the next class. "I'm home," people say, over and over.

As the period of grant funding comes to a close, we will begin to fund our Minister of Outreach ourselves. Laura Ruth will continue to help us attract newcomers, minister to their needs, and develop new programs internally so that they can find their place, share their gifts.

We will further develop our advertising and other publicity materials, rolling out a lean, beautiful brochure, putting up new exterior signage and developing space for public use on our front lawn, and capitalizing on media outreach opportunities in Somerville and beyond: Twitter, community blogs, underwriting on public radio.

Our aim is to increase our visibility in the community—to make First Church a household name—as well as to migrate our culture toward one in which we are comfortable inviting our friends and others to church.

Your pledge at work might make way for:

- A transplant from the Midwest who finds himself in the frosty Northeast. He doesn't know a soul in town, but finds us on the Internet, and makes friends the first day.
- A straight couple who didn't know a church like ours existed, until they walked by and saw the prayer box and the rainbow flag. They now know that "religious progressive" is not an oxymoron.
- Someone who's newly sober or newly separated, or someone who finds herself depressed every December. They are invited to church by one of our ministers, or by you, and find a home.

Every day, people like these move to our community who need a church like ours—will they hear about us?

Budget total: $59,280

(Includes a percentage of the pastors' salary; the pastors' utilities, expenses and insurance; the secretary, growth budget, communications team budget, telephone, internet, copier, insurance maintenance and utilities)

To do the work of justice that Jesus asks us to be partners in, for the healing of the world.

In 2009, buoyed by the prophetic call of your chair of finance, First Church gave away more than in perhaps any previous year: 8% of our pledges went to our mission and justice partners, and 9% went to Our Church's Wider Mission to support the UCC's work throughout the state, country and world. Many of our mission and justice partners expressed how moved they were that a church would increase instead of decrease their giving in a recession. While corporate and individual charitable giving fell dramatically, increasing the financial strain of places like the Somerville Homeless Coalition and the Casa San Jose orphanage, we acted counterintuitively. We gave out of faith, not out of fear.

This year, we won the Steve Burton prize for the team that raised the most funds in the Homeless Coalition's 5k race. We were the only community partner of RESPOND, Somerville's domestic violence shelter, an agency that served over 5,000 women this year. Our Casa San Jose mission team will pay for their travel expenses out-of-pocket so that the proceeds of all of our fundraisers go to the orphanage.

We donated time as well as money. You volunteered as mentors for teenage girls who are clients of Somerville Mental Health association. You cooked and served a weekly meal for the hungry at our church, and a monthly meal at the College Ave shelter: home-cooked, nourishing, lovingly prepared meals.

In the year to come, we propose giving a full tithe: 10% to our mission partners and 10% to Our Church's Wider Mission, to support the church's work in the world, the work of feeding the hungry, sheltering the naked, releasing the prisoner from captivity. More and more, we are giving and acting visibly, the way Christians are supposed to, on behalf of the world's wounded places.

Your pledge at work might make way for:

- An unemployed Iraq war vet who turned to drugs to erase the images of war from his mind. When he leaves detox, he finds emergency shelter with the help of the Somerville Homeless Coalition.
- A smart and motivated Mexican teenager who is also grindingly poor. Casa San Jose orphanage pays for his English classes, which open vocational doors.
- African clergy who confront the homophobia and internalized racism that swept in with the HIV epidemic. INERELA funds their efforts to transform the cultural and religious landscape of AIDS in Africa.

Alone, we feel so helpless against these huge social problems. Together, we make a significant difference, and fulfill Christ's call to serve "the least of these," who embody Him.

Budget total: $63,840 (This total includes the Mission and Justice budget, a percentage of the pastors' salary; the pastors' utilities, expenses and insurance; the church administrator, telephone, internet, copier, insurance maintenance and utilities)

Total needed to fulfill our 2010 mission of Walking in the Way of Jesus: $228,000

Increase in pledges necessary to meet the needs of our spiritual budget: $40,000 (a 37% increase over last year)

A detailed line-item budget is available from the chair of Finance, by emailing XXXXX or calling XXXXX.

Wordle

(see next page)

WORDLE LETTER

Beloved Community,

The visual budget on the other side of this page represents an (admittedly non-scientific) word picture of what your pledge dollars support. We have moved from decades of deficit budgets to our first year in the black, 2009. We have moved from scarcity—keeping our resources for ourselves—to abundance, giving the first 18% of our pledges away to community need and wider church support.

In eight years we have grown from a staff of two, to a staff of 10 part-time people, all working hard to make our church a place where God is real and Jesus is alive and well. All this is a result of your freehanded, faithful giving.

The 2012 First Church Somerville budget is still a work-in-progress, depending on your generosity.

- A 15% increase in pledges over 2011 would fund a bare-bones budget with no deficit, but no raises
- A 25% increase in pledges would get us to a compromise budget with a reasonably small deficit
- A 30% increase in pledges would get us to our dream budget, with all programs and staff fully funded and fairly compensated

Beloved, please hang this visual budget on your fridge, pray over it, talk to your partner and kids if you have them, about what your church means to you. How big is #FirstChurchSomerville in the tag cloud of your life?

Love,

Molly

CityMissionSociety
Preaching
Meals
HungerRelief
LGBTsafeSpace
ArtSunday
Faith
GodlyPlay
BlockParty
Respond
SomervilleHomelessCoalition
EqualExchange
Laughter
Survivors
Soup
Shelter
WiderUCC
Community
Foolish
People
Warmth
Useful
BlessingoftheAnimals
ImmigrationRights
Support
Education
ProjectHaveHope
Retreat
MusicMinisters
ChildCare
Prayer
FairTradeCoffee
Service
Justice
Light
Baptism
SomervilleMentalHealth
re/New
Tomatoes
Teachers
PastoralCare
Music
Parents'NightOut
DisasterRelief
Orphans
UrbanGarden
LaughinginChurch
RooftopPeople
HolyFriends
ChurchWorldService
Bread
ArtBeat
Basil
DieselHours
Recovery
Song
Yoga
Joyful
CentroPresente
Immigrants
SpiritualBooks
Antipoverty
SacredConversationsonRace
Beloved
MexicanOrphans
FlyingHedgehogs
Rest
PublicArt
Insurance
DragGospelBrunch
Copier
Meditation
Candles

Two Sermons on Money:

Here's a sermon one of our laypeople preached, when we were just starting conversations about money and transparency. It's excellent spiritual advice! I think she should preach it again every year.

Get Your Grandma and Grandpa On!

About five years ago, just around Lent and right after Simon was born, my husband and I started to think about our long-term goals. We were married less than a year, living in a cheap apartment in Chelsea, and dreaming of owning our own place. I was working full time, going to grad school at night. And David was home with Simon. We were a few months into being a one-income family and we talked about talking about our finances and budgeting but we just never got around to it. Talking about money gave me the heeby jeebies. What if we weren't on the same page? What if David thought something that I "needed" was frivolous and judged me? What if he thought I was judging him? Besides, there was cash in our bank account. It wasn't like we couldn't buy the things we wanted. Sure we both had some credit card debt and we each had our own cars —a Toyota Corolla and Matrix—not exactly super high end. And I had taken a low interest loan on my 401k to pay for part of our wedding. I figured I would just be paying forever anyway and why not enjoy life a little. Someday I would have a super high-paying job and *poof* everything would magically go away.

So we had debt, I knew it wasn't good, but I really didn't want to know how bad it was.

You ready to hear? Wait for it…

We had six…try seven thousand dollars in high interest debt. $97,000 if you included my "good debt" student loans. 67 thousand dollars! That was twice my salary!

I was angry. Angry at myself; I felt so much shame; the weight of all this debt. I'd become an indentured servant to credit card companies.

We sat in my living room going over the overwhelming list of debt and made some tough decisions. Yet, for the first time in a very long time I actually was relieved. Certainly not because of the amount of debt I accumulated (I was pretty embarrassed about that) but because I knew. I now could see exactly what was in front of us. Just as Laura Ruth preached last week: "We started practicing living in the light. We're trying to find all the dark places in our lives and let a little light in there." Oh and did we shine the light on that one.

One of my favorite sayings I picked up from a mentor is "The news is the news." It isn't "good or bad," it's the news. We interpret it as good or bad. Once you have the news, then you can actually *do* something about it. Although doing something about it is sometimes easier said than done.

A couple weeks ago Molly gave us suggestions on how we can invite the Christian Lenten practices into our lives through: praying, fasting, and almsgiving. More specifically, she said we could "give alms to the poor: think energy bars in your backpack, dollar bills for the Spare Change folks. To pray: we have handouts at the back of the church for new and simple ways to add prayer to your daily life . . . .To fast: you can take on giving something up, a lesser god whom you are done obeying, to make room for the One God."

So what if we applied these three spiritual practices with our financial practices?

Let's talk about giving alms for a minute. If you are in a similar situation as I was and in debt to your eyeballs, living paycheck to paycheck, you might not feel like you have a dollar to spare, but like me you probably have a lot of "stuff." For me, seeing all my "stuff" was a constant reminder of how I got into this mess. One of the most cleansing experiences I had was boxing up and donating clothes and books and right-sizing my "stuff" while I right-sized my financials.

In the scripture reading today Jesus said, "Take care! Be on your guard against all kinds of greed; for one's life does not consist in the abundance of possessions." Then he told them a parable: "The land of a rich man produced abundantly. And he thought to himself, 'What should I do, for I have no place to store my crops?' Then he said, 'I will do this: I will pull down my barns and build larger ones, and there I will store all my grain and my goods." Doesn't this remind you of the George Carlin skit on "Stuff"? Your house is a place to store all your stuff so you can go out and buy more stuff! Here is this rich man who has an abundance of possessions. I imagine these things and managing these things consume his thoughts. I mean, he's adding to his stockpile and now wants to tear down his storage to build a bigger storage. And why does he need to store it, is he afraid it won't be replaced? Can you imagine how much time, effort and energy it takes to live like that? What if the rich man gave away some of those crops instead of building bigger and bigger places to store his stuff? What if we did the same? How much freer would we feel? Right-sizing not only de-cluttered my home, but it de-cluttered my soul! Give till it feels good!

The second practice is prayer. No, I'm not going to suggest we add "prayers to win the lottery" during the prayers for the people. But I do think that money-type prayers can be part of Lenten prayer practice.

Here is the thing about money. Money is just a tool. Just like the "news is the news," it is how we interpret it; how we use it. Yet, money issues can be so deeply rooted, we may not even be aware of how money or talking about money or using, spending or obsessing over money affects us. Many of our attitudes about money come from our parents and our upbringing. Maybe you heard things like:

- Money burns a hole in my pocket.
- I can't afford to pursue the career I want.
- Women don't make as much money as men.
- If you want something you have to be willing to sacrifice.
- Don't carry cash, you'll either spend it or someone will clunk you over the head and take it.
- Maybe you heard, if we only waited longer before having kids?
- Maybe your parents constantly fought about money.
- Or maybe they never talked about money around you at all.

Becoming aware of your attitudes about money and recognizing how these beliefs influence your relationship with others and with money can help you work through these challenging issues. The first step to overcoming your fear is awareness. This is where prayer comes in.

In the book *Healing the Eight Stages of Life,* Linns and Fabricant offer a wonderful way of visualizing prayer. They call it "Prayer of Creative Imagination." There are four parts that can be used for healing any hurtful experience, not just around money:

1. Recall a time when you felt deeply loved. Re-experience that scene breathing that love into yourself again.
2. Now recall a time when you were hurt. Maybe it was around money. Re-experience it using all of your senses to imagine it. Maybe you are sitting around the dinner table and your parents are tired and angry and fighting about money. Get in touch with the feelings.
3. Let Jesus join the scene. Watch what he says and does for you, watch how he adds to the conversation.
4. Breathe in all the ways Jesus is loving you, and breathe out any hurt.

The third Lenten practice is fasting: Molly suggested, "you can take on giving something up, a lesser god whom you are done obeying, to make room for the

One God." One idea is to live like your grandma and grandpa did. What do I mean by that? I mean the basics: Use cash. Not too much. Practice gratitude. Can you tell I've been reading Michael Pollan too? Live in financial transparency. Shine the light on it.

But what if you are in debt? Or scared to find out just how much debt you have? Or not sure how to create a budget? Start simple.

Here is a basic way of practicing value-based budgeting: Either by yourself or with your partner, or your whole family . . . start having those healthy conversations about money now! List out all of your basic needs (e.g. food, shelter, clothing—things we can't live without). And I say basic to challenge, do we really need two phones, a land line and a cell? or a data plan? or cable tv? Basic needs are just that, basic. Basic needs are taken off the top of the income side. Now brainstorm and list what you value: church, organic produce, family time, reading, education, cable, retirement, bigger apartment with a second bathroom, second car, living debt-free. Most likely these values are very close to your "wants." You could survive without them, but they do make life more joyful. Here is the fun part. Once you have your list—take 100 pennies—exactly 100 pennies, and put whatever number of pennies you would place on each value. If you only have 100 pennies, how much would you spend on church, organic produce, family vacations . . . .You see where I am going with this? You've just created a percentage-based budget that reflects your core values.

Here are some other tips you may have heard but are definitely worth repeating:

- If you have debt, pay off the highest interest rate first
- Call periodically to try to get your rates lowered
- Pay cash
- Freeze your assets (put your credit card in water and freeze it in the freezer. If it is worth buying, it is worth waiting for the card to melt!)
- Always pay your bills on time
- Consider becoming a one-car household or a no-car household. We became a one-car household and saved not only in car payment, insurance and gas, but on all the things that we didn't buy because we *didn't* have the second car.
- Contribute to your 401k or pension plan (especially if your employer matches). Do this *even if you have debt* otherwise you will be leaving money on the table.
- If you receive an unexpected monetary gift, put some toward your debt and some to your savings

- Give back—try percent-based giving, even if you are in debt
- Practice an attitude of gratitude
- Open a high-interest savings account
- Pay more on your mortgage each month to shave off years
- Track your spending (write everything down for a week/month/during Lent)
- If you have a credit card, get a dividend card that gives cash back and always pay the balance in full
- Go one day without spending any money
- Go one week without using your credit card
- Go one month without eating out
- Create a six-month savings reserve
- Set a SMART goal around money (specific, measurable, attainable, realistic and timely)
- Remember, you didn't get in debt overnight, so don't expect to get out of debt overnight either: simple shifts
- Find a buddy in church to help you keep you accountable

Lastly, just because my mom is here and I had to get her in my sermon as payback for all the times I was in hers—practice what she always said to us: "Think before you do."

These simple shifts do add up. Just over a year ago, we officially got out of debt, continue to contribute 15% to retirement, give 8% away and slowly built up a six-month reserve fund. Shining the light on our debt and making some simple shifts took away the worry and is such a wonderfully freeing experience for mind, body and soul.

As for our dream of owning a home . . . we were blessed to qualify for affordable housing and bought a right-sized home with our right-sized income last January.

Eckhart Tolle in *The Power of Now* writes, "When you are full of problems, there is no room for anything new to enter, no room for a solution. So whenever you can, make some room, create some space so that you find the life underneath your life situation."

Find a way to shift your thinking and imbue your life with gratitude. Focus on your breathing and connect with God. Know you are safe, loved and there is abundance all around you.

Here's a sermon I preached on tithing—a new frontier for a lot of my people, who have only recently gotten on board with the idea of pledging. Onward and upward! I got a lot of good verbal feedback from people on this sermon—and a huge leap in the number of people who self-identified as tithers, from 15 to 30% of our pledging units.

"Waiting for the Gift"

Deuteronomy 14:22-26, Malachi 3:10

This is a love story.

I remember the first time I knew that I was home, really home, here at First Church.

It was my first coffee hour here as your pastor, and it was ten years ago this weekend. We were a much smaller church then, but we took coffee hour just as seriously.

I had grown up in church and loved church. Otherwise I would not have become a pastor. But all the churches of which I'd been a part, either as a kid in Sunday school or a student minister in seminary or a greenhorn associate pastor, had a retro quality to them. It was like walking back in time to walk into a church: from the hairdos on the church ladies to the lemon squares on the table. It was comforting, this otherworldliness, because let's face it: the world can be too hard sometimes. Just too hard, and we want to escape to a time that seemed simpler, even if that time is itself a fiction we've created.

Then, First Church Somerville. My first coffee hour: and I noticed, on the table, lemon squares—Dibbie's lemon squares. And takeout sushi. Which is a pretty good summary of our congregation, still.

Our church, and that coffee hour, is the first time I had ever experienced God in church as a God of the present and the near future—not just the God of a fictionalized past. And I fell, hard, for this God and this church.

We have had a lot of meals together since then. There was the first time we had our Maundy Thursday Last Supper, feeling awkward and shy to eat in the sanctuary but eager at the same time, at the long table in front of the chancel, and Deacon Gary who is at heart a mystic and not all that attentive to the clock brought hard-boiled eggs for the table that turned out to be raw in the middle.

There was the awesome wild rave we had for our capital campaign kickoff, at

The Living Room in the North End, drinking champagne and eating lobster and raw oysters, living as if we were robber barons but knowing that this was God's doing, that for one night we were to eat like princes, and then come home to feed the paupers again.

We've eaten Mardi Gras pancakes with Catholic Mexican orphans and eaten cross-free Palm Sunday hot cross buns with Unitarians. Our feasting does not discriminate.

I remember other meals from the last ten years: meals that arrived to the parsonage next door, private meals for hard times, meals to ease our family's suffering, but I could taste the love of an entire people in them. Kim brought her lasagna when I lost my mother. Quiche when I had a miscarriage, and then another miscarriage. And, that fall when I was in chemo and things were really, really bad: every week, another quart of butternut squash soup from a different parishioner. It still tasted like love, but I never want to see a pot of butternut squash soup again in my life.

Food is how we celebrate, and how we move beyond grief and decide to keep living. And when we bring it into the house of God, it's our way of showing up and showing love for God and for one another. Manna doesn't fall from heaven anymore—it comes off of supermarket shelves and from the stoves and ovens of people in this community who have decided they also want to be the hands of God in this place, whether or not that's how they think of themselves, because they're too modest.

Unlike ancient Israel, the tithe of our harvest is completely voluntary. Some of you might have felt otherwise when Rev. Jeff assigned you to a coffee klatch last year, but in the UCC, this whole enterprise only works because you decide to show up and commit your substance. Without you, it would all fall apart. There is no sugar daddy, no mother church, and precious little endowment. What we have on our table is there because you all brought it. And what we have in our church checking account is there because you gave it away.

It is not an easy thing to decide to tithe, to part with a significant chunk of your hard-earned money. It can be almost physically painful, and also terrifying. For this reason, I think, the authors of Deuteronomy and Malachi overstated the case a little bit—they employed a little hyperbole to convince us to part with our cash, and also incentivized us, or, put less nicely, bribed us.

"With the money secure in hand, go to the place that the Lord your God will choose. Spend the money for whatever you wish! Oxen, sheep, wine, strong drink, or whatever you desire."

Wait. What? Is the Bible really telling us that we are to hand over 10% of our earnings to the Lord—and then telling us we can turn it into a catered meal, and eat it all up again? And not only that, I think, correct me if I'm wrong—did that just say we can get drunk in church, with the offering money? Wahoo! Tequila shots at coffee hour, on me!

And then there's the Malachi reading, in which God says "bring the full tithe into the storehouse, so that there may be food in my house, and thus put me to the test: see if I will not open the windows of heaven for you and pour down for you an overflowing blessing." These were words spoken to the ancient Jews, whose ancestors had experienced firsthand just such a thing—manna coming from heaven, daily bread, when they were starving in the wilderness.

In other words: this is an airtight argument for the tithe. God is saying: you can't lose. If you bring a tenth of your income and harvest to God's temple, not only will you get to eat it up before you go on home, God will keep on blessing you after you leave. This is a money-back guarantee. Which is a little unbelievable. If it were believable, really trustworthy, we would all be doing it already. But we're not.

So your church is making it believable, we are co-signing this scripture with a real money back guarantee. I told you a few weeks ago, and renew that invitation today—if you tithe at least 5% of your income to your church, and you do not notice a significant shift in your spiritual life over the next year, you can have your money back. All you have to do is ask.

This is not hyperbole, and it's not a gimmick. It's a carrot, yes. We're offering it not because of our need to balance the budget—we're offering it because those of us who already tithe know that our lives have been changed, and we suspect that giving radically and biblically was somehow fundamental to the change. We want everyone to have the freedom to take that same step, and find out for themselves.

What if there were things God couldn't give us unless we tithed? The Deuteronomy scripture goes on to say that we shall bring out our tithes so that the Lord your God may bless you in all the work you undertake. Are there things we are holding on to so tightly that we can't receive anything new?

Tithing is a spiritual exercise in handing our lives back to God, in opening the hand to receive as well as give. We practice giving our substance away, over and over, so that by the end of our earthly life it's easy to let go entirely. You may have known someone, a beloved grandparent or other elderly person who was a hoarder. The more stuff they had, the more anchored they felt. It made them safe. But when they died, they died hard.

I know it's difficult to think about giving a lot of money away, and not worry about your own needs. I know it's hard to give money away and not think of where it's going, whether the place and people it's going to are worthy, whether they will do as good a job with it as you would. Churches all around us are dying, running out of money and winking out like old candles burned all the way down, and it's because people don't believe in them; somewhere along the way, the trust broke down. The people's faith in churches, if not in God, has gone away, if this generation ever had it, and the coffers and the coffee hour tables are empty.

And maybe churches, even ours, aren't totally worthy of the tithe. I'll say it. Even in our church, when you hand over your money, how can you be sure, really sure, that it's well spent? That we have the lowest overhead and the highest impact? And another thing: knowing some of your money passes through this place and goes on to the Somerville Homeless Coalition or to RESPOND, well, wouldn't it be more efficient just to give directly?

Yes. But maybe that's not the point. Our tithes, when they pass through this place, they change. They get hope attached to them, they get prayers stuck on them, and then they leave again. Our God is not efficient. We don't pray to God and say, "Oh Most Competent Ruler of the Universe." That's not what we look for in God. Or if we do look for that in our God, we might not like Her if we actually met Her.

Maybe it's easier to think of it like this. The meals you remember are not the most efficient meals. You don't reminisce aloud with friends, "Remember the time we ate our frozen burritos in 30 seconds flat? That was awesome!" "Hey do you remember a time when we didn't even bother to heat them up! We didn't even take the wrapper off! That was a great meal. Let's do that again sometime." We don't remember meals we ate efficiently and we don't, as a rule, remember meals we ate alone. Something had to happen to those meals for them to be memorable—there had to be love at the table. Or surprises. Or strangers who became friends, or were unmasked as angels. These are the memorable meals. These are the holy meals.

And it's the same with our money, which is just our harvest feast turned into something we can carry around in a checkbook. Someone said that tithing gives an outward form to an inward remembering: that God has been with us every step of the way. When our ancestors were farmers and ranchers, we understood that it was God who had made the rain rain and the sun shine and the animals thrive. And even now when we are so distant from our agrarian roots, some of us, hopefully a lot of us, can see how God has brought us good things, and so we remember by giving a portion back to God. We carry it to the table, we and our household rejoicing together.

This week I sent you an article from a colleague, Lillian Daniel. Mired in credit card and student loan debt, she swore she would never tithe, and resented her better-paid senior minister for even suggesting it. Then she heard a voice from God, telling her to do it, and telling her if she did, she would get a gift. She sat back and waited for it.

I went through exactly the same arc as Lillian. I felt that way at my previous churches. Easy for you to say, senior minister with your healthy retirement account and student loans paid off.

But at some point, my fear and resentment shifted. Love shifted it. I became personally invested in the vision here. And I began to see the benefit of giving a tithe. It was easy to see what was in it for me—it came directly back to me as lemon squares and sushi, and even butternut squash soup.

But also somewhere along the way, it stopped being about my own hungers; it became about seeing other people fed; that's what fed me. This was the gift I had been waiting for, but I didn't know it at the time. I often don't make it to the coffee hour table in time, but I am never hungry, because I see what is happening. I see you holding the wrong babies, and pulling shy people in from the sidelines, and becoming family to people who have no one who loves them the way they should be loved, and I'm full, full, full. Maybe you feel this way too. I feel like I can't lose, and I never have here, not yet.

Sermon on Sex

Rev. Molly Baskette

"Cardinal Sins: Lust"

I Corinthians 6:12-20

The Greco Roman world didn't see much of a connection between sex and religion.

Maybe it should have stayed that way!

On the other hand, Paul was trying to establish some ground rules in an environment that didn't have any—most of the Corinthian Christians were not converted Jews, who would have had a lot of rules about sex, but Gentiles, or non-Jews. Had to figure out what was permitted, and what was not permitted. You might even make the case that Paul was a feminist: since the sex norms of the day—which included man-boy love, rape in war, and sex outside of the economically stabilizing institution of marriage in a time before contraception, benefited men, but not necessarily women or children.

Some of the phrases you will hear, if finger quotes had been invented, would have been around then. Corinth, was big on slogans—another reminder of Vegas.

And so we have arrived at the fifth in our Lenten series on the cardinal sins, Lust. Insert nervous laughter here.

It might be easier to solve the problem of lust than we think. Pope Gregory, who refined the list of cardinal sins down to the seven we've inherited, didn't say we weren't to have sex. He said we were to avoid lust. So we should be able to do whatever we want in bed, as long as we don't enjoy it.

Except that doesn't seem like something that God, who invented the orgasm, could possibly want for us, either.

I wonder how many times the word orgasm has been uttered in this sanctuary in the 100 years it has stood here. Orgasm! Orgasm! My guess is, four times. Does anyone here still doubt that we need to talk about sex in church? Hear this. While the claim that men think about sex every seven seconds has been widely disproved, some reliable studies show that men do think about sex on average 19 times a day, and women, 10 times a day. I ask you: how many times a day do you think about, say, substitutionary atonement? Or the theology of the trinity?

Until you are thinking about those 19 times a day, I think we preachers should preach somewhat more proportionally about sex, something you actually think about and maybe have some issues around in your daily life. Which puts me about a thousand sermons behind, for this calendar year alone.

Maybe I can sneak in a couple of microsermons, with guidance from our Holy Scripture.

Sermon on adultery: Israel's King David lusted after Bathsheba when he spied her bathing from a rooftop. They did the nasty, and he ordered her husband, Uriah the Hittite, into the most dangerous area of Israel's next battle. Uriah died, naturally, and David married Bathsheba, resulting in the birth of his son Solomon, and no permanent loss of status as God's favorite. Moral of the story: adultery is just one of those things that comes with the territory of being a charismatic leader.

Sermon on masturbation: in Genesis, Onan was ordered, according to Hebrew law, to impregnate his widowed sister-in-law, to carry on the male line. He refused, and instead spilled his seed onto the ground, an offense for which God put him to death. Moral of the story: any sex that doesn't result in more babies for our now overcrowded planet is a capital offense.

Sermon on polyamory, also from Genesis: when Sarah couldn't get pregnant because of her advanced age, she encouraged her husband Abraham to have sex with her house-slave Hagar. She knew how to keep her man. Only it backfired on her: when Hagar got pregnant, she lorded it over Sarah, and shamed her, and Sarah wanted her dead. Moral of the story: don't boink where you eat. Come to think of it, this might actually still be good advice.

Ok, so, Old Testament stories might not make us less confused about what constitutes healthy sex, it turns out. Though they do remind us that sex, while a gift from God, has always been complicated and corrupted by humans and their secrets and power-plays and pride. We could go see what Jesus has to say, but a warning: he is not the easy teacher. He was the one who said that if we even lust in our hearts for someone who is married, we have committed adultery.

Which brings us back to Paul, the other major voice in the New Testament, and his encouragement to honor God with our bodies.

I wonder what Paul would have said about some of the 21st century problems we have invented around sex and desire? The Internet has given us whole new ways to abuse the privilege of having bodies and having desires in those bodies.

Rafe heard about a website from a friend at school—it was supposed to be a site on making your own comic strip, called oogle.com. Only when he entered the keystrokes and missed a critical letter, he stumbled across a site helping local Somervillians find hot anonymous boink buddies. Needless to say, he was surprised. We are not more sexually sinful than we were in 2000 BC, but we are certainly more efficient at sinning: for example, how many extramarital affairs has Facebook launched since inception? Someone who might have remained simply lonely or frustrated in their marriage, who might have fantasized about cheating but would not have gone looking for it, now has easy means to an emotional or an actual affair right in their living room.

The pendulum has always swung back and forth in human sexual behavior and mores. The strictness of I Corinthians was Paul's answer to the free-love good times of Corinth, which were not good for everybody. The Summer of Love ended the 60s, the AIDS crisis inaugurated the 80s. For millennia we have been oscillating back and forth between no boundaries and lots of boundaries, trying to figure out what the sweet spot is, what constitutes healthy and good sex.

I'm going to take a stab at a definition of good sex: Good sex is sex that is good for everybody involved. We are progressive Christians who understand that everything we do has consequences beyond what we can see—we are linked in invisible spiritual and physical networks, and we know that our decisions matter. We consider this in how we drive, eat, work, buy. Why not consider this in how we sex, as well?

The other night at House Church, we crowdsourced a working definition of healthy sexuality. Two of the men in our group took things in a beautiful direction. "Why is it," one of them wondered aloud, "that in our culture we tend to talk about purity only in terms of virginity? It's either/or. Once you lose your virginity, we say that that 'pure' is gone. I'd like to see us develop a concept for purity that goes along with growing up as sexual people—the idea that we get more pure as we get older, as we learn what our partners want, as we become more generous lovers, as we learn to communicate clearly our needs and boundaries, as we commit to radical honesty and tenderness, as we make peace with our bodies, though they are imperfect, and learn to love them as they are." The other man at our table burst in, "We could call it the Sex: It Gets Better campaign!"

The Holy Spirit was with us in that moment of conversation. It makes so much sense! If we as Christians are the kind of people who want to be in tune with God and everything God has made in regard to how we eat and work and buy, why would sex be in a different category? Shouldn't sex work the same way as everything else—shouldn't we be able to get holier as sexual people, the older we get and the more we practice healthy sex? Did you know that most people in sex therapy are young people? Do you suppose this is a coincidence?

Paul said that we should let people see God in and through our bodies. There are virgins in this room, and there are people who have been around the block, and there are people who have been around the whole city. There are people who are locked up inside, sexually speaking, who have never really enjoyed the gift of sexuality, and there are people who have violated boundaries and hurt themselves and others. The first thing I want to say is: every one of you is precious to God. The second thing I want to say is: lots of us have done things in regard to our bodies that we feel badly about now. We may even feel badly about things someone else did to us, even though it was not our fault. These choices have had a deep physical or emotional impact on ourselves or someone else, in the form of STDs, unwanted pregnancies, emotional residue.

I am here to tell you that wherever you've been and whatever you've done: you are forgiven, and today is a new day, and it's yours, and you have tomorrow too, and you have every other day for the rest of your life, to have better sex. Sex is a spiritual practice like any other, and we are called to let others see God by the kind of sex we have. Though probably not literally called to let them see. That might violate a boundary. And along with that I remind you that some of the best and safest sex we can have is sex by ourselves: fantasy, touch, dance, loving the body God entrusted to us.

For these bodies do belong to God. The Greeks and Romans weren't so big on the body: their various schools of philosophy said that because bodies were just temporary shells, we either had to beat their hungers and desires into submission, or we could do whatever we felt like with them. They were ascetics or libertines. But Paul taught us that like Jesus, we will be resurrected when death takes us, in the body, so what we do with our bodies now matters greatly.

(start Shakira's Waka Waka song at 1:30) My favorite teacher of preaching says that the best sermons have a long start and a quick finish. Kind of like the best sex. When we were in Mexico over February vacation, the Baskettes went into town on a random Tuesday afternoon, for an ice cream cone. Only we'd forgotten it was Mardi Gras, and downtown was shut down for the Mardi Gras parade. In Colima, the kings and queens of Mardi Gras are not the town beauties. They are not young women, oiled and blushed and coiled and curled to perfection. The people marching in the parade are almost exclusively the old women, and a few old men, of the surrounding villages. The little old ladies of Coquimatlan were in handmade Carmen Miranda outfits, every last one, with slits up to there, and fruit hats on their sometimes toothless heads, and they were dancing. They were dancing to Shakira's Waka Waka. And they were shaking what God gave them, shaking breasts that had nursed babies decades before, shaking bottoms round with rice and beans! They were shaking it like Shakira! And loving every inch of themselves! And we couldn't help but love them too! Every face lining that street was smiling, and every body dancing with them, in glorious unity! One flesh! That is what it means to let others see God in and through our bodies.

Liturgist Guidelines for Sunday Worship

- Read the scripture for that Sunday early in the week, and let the Holy Spirit work on it in you
- Please send a draft of your liturgy for review to the preacher of the week by Friday at 5:00pm. The preacher will comment on structure but will not edit for content (that is, will not tell you your feelings or ideas are "wrong")
- Submit final (or nearly final) version of your liturgy for review by 5:00pm on Saturday
- Come twenty minutes before worship on Sunday, so you can pray with the worship leaders in the chapel and get settled
- Don't be afraid of the microphone—speak up!
- Remember what a sacred trust it is to be allowed to speak from the chancel. Be mindful of children present, of the diversity of our congregation.
- Reserve hot-button issues unrelated to the theme of the day for a church forum where there is an opportunity for dialogue

Invitation to confession: No more than one page, double-spaced. Read from the lectern, on the chancel.

Always begin by saying "Now is the time when we bring our own stories before God."

The invitation should be confessional, humble before God, an opportunity to reveal your own vulnerability and fallen-ness. You should not reveal an open wound, lest you put the congregation in the position of needing to minister to you, but a wound that is healing, a wound around which you have some sense of God's grace at work already. Liturgists often tell a personal story at this time. An effective invitation to confession is a bit of a cliffhanger: it sets up the problem ("where I felt apart from God, broken or hurt, where I fell short of God's grace") but doesn't offer the solution. The **assurance of grace** (see below) will do this work.

You should read the scripture for the day carefully in preparing your own words, as well as ruminate on the preacher's theme. You should not, under any circumstances, talk about "something else that has been on your mind." The faithful movement of the Holy Spirit depends on your careful listening to scripture and thoughtfulness about the preacher's topic for the day. This does not mean you need to agree with the preacher's opinion, only that you need to hew closely to the theme.

Keep in mind that when the congregation hears your confession, they have not yet heard the scripture for the day (though they may have read it while waiting for worship to begin). It's important to reference the scripture accordingly, giving a little brief context.

After the invitation, you lead people in the **unison prayer** (nice and slow, loud enough so they can hear you as a guide, but not so loud you're shouting them down). It's also good to break up long sentences into shorter phrases with pauses, so people can catch up. [Note: the preacher for the day will prepare the unison prayer, and send it to you ahead of time]

After this there is a period of **silent confession**—you can just be prayerful yourself, or if you feel the need to track the time so it's not too much and not too little, you can silently recite the Lord's Prayer.

Assurance of Grace: A few sentences.

The assurance of grace should deal with how your situation got resolved: where was God in this? Where is redemption, connection to God? Where is the grace, and how can we get some? The assurance of grace is a reminder that it doesn't matter where we've been or what we've done, God forgives all of our sin, our separation from God, ourselves, others. It should link back into the story you told in the invitation, and "wrap it up" or bring it home: demonstrate grace, insight, healing, responsiveness from God.

Remember: the assurance of grace is not just "the end of the story, how it all worked out," but specifically 1) how God entered the story, and 2) how God will enter all of our stories in this way—if we let Her. Generalize the assurance to us so we can believe it for ourselves, and **be sure that God is a named character in the story.**

Invitation to Offering: No more than 2 or 3 sentences. Spoken from the Communion table, on the floor, with the cordless mic.

This piece may also draw on themes from the scripture or sermon. We remind people in specific ways why it is important, practically and spiritually, to give to our church, and end it by saying: "the offering will now be received." Liturgists often use humor to make a point, so feel free to do so, if the spirit moves you in that direction.

After you speak, the organist plays offering music, collectors collect, and children bring collection plates forward during the sung response. **They hold the plates** while you bless the offering, with hands held out toward the plates, palm down.

Prayer of Dedication: One or two sentences

This is the one form of your liturgy that addresses God, and not the people. Ask God to bless the offering to God's own purposes.

After you offer the prayer, take the plates from the children and place them on the altar, underneath the cross at the back of the chancel.

Guest Card

We're so glad you've come to First Church Somerville.
If you would like to let us know about you, will you fill out this card and place it in the offering plate?

Date ____________________ Name: ________________________________

Name(s) & Age(s) of Child(ren), if any: ______________________________

____

When you're ready for a permanent nametag, please write your name as you'd like it to appear: ____

Give yourself a snazzy title! Totally optional (but fun!): ____________________

____

Email address: ____

_____ I'd like to receive the once-a-week First Church email to keep me up on the most important happenings and announcements.

_____ I'd like to join the community listerv–I'll be able to receive and send emails with the larger community about things in and out of church.

_____ I'd like to join the young adult listserv to keep up on the happenings of the 20s-30s crowd.

_____ I'd like to join the parents listserv to keep up on Sunday School and kid stuff.

How did you hear about the church?

____

What do you love to do? Have you done it in a church or organization before?

____

Cell phone: ____

Home phone: ____

Mailing Address: ____

____

Prayer Request

First Church Somerville's **Pastoral Prayer Team** will be honored to pray the prayers of our heart this week with you.

Please write your prayer request here and place it in the offering plate.

if you are interested in becoming a member of the Pastoral Prayer Team, please email Christy at XXXXXXXX.

FIRST CHURCH
SOMERVILLE UCC

Seek first the Kingdom of God and God's righteousness, and all these things will be given to you as well.
Matthew 6:33

Pledged Commitment for 2013

Name(s) ______________________________
____
Email ______________________________
Address ______________________________
____
____
City ______________ State ________ Zip ________

☐ $10/Week ☐ $25/Week ☐ $50/Week ☐ $75/Week ☐ $100/Week

☐ Other Amount: ____ per: ☐ Week ☐ Month

☐ Other (please describe):______________________________

☐ My pledge amount represents a tithe (5-10% of my take home pay)

☐ Please do not share my pledge amount with the pastors of First Church

First Church Somerville By the Numbers: 2012

New hymnals bought and dedicated: 30
Marching bands rebooted: 1!
Miles flown in support of the Casa San Jose orphanage: 70,392
Percentage increase in worship attendees: 40%
Total number of children in church school: 56
$10 gift cards given to local folks in need: 167
Honk!fest folks our kitchen fed: 650
Sermons preached outdoors: 6
Percentage increase in Drag Queens and Kings at DGF2: 120%
Angels at Occupy Bethlehem: 9
Home visits for Defying Gravity Capital Campaign: 111
Percentage by which we smashed our Campaign goal: 19% (for a total of $595,007 in pledges)
First Churchers who were the Face of God in the Pride Parade, Honk!fest and Artbeat: 62
Pastors arrested for civil disobedience on behalf of the 99%: 1
First Churchers who identify their annual pledge as a tithe of their income: 30%

What could God do with this church if we **all** gave a percentage of our income?

FIRST CHURCH SOMERVILLE UCC

Building the Beloved Community

Epiphany

February 23, 2014 | **Seventh Sunday after Epiphany** | **9:00 and 11:00 A.M.**

Prelude Savior, Like a Shepherd Lead Us *Tune: BRADBURY, arr. Paul Tate*

***Hymn #70** God Is Here! As We Your People Meet

Call to Worship and Welcome

ONE: God is good!

ALL: All the time!

Passing of the Peace

ONE: The peace of Christ be with you.

ALL: And also with you.

A Time of Confession Marcus Mack

Invitation to Confession

Unison Prayer of Confession

Make me an instrument of Your peace;
Forgive my trespasses of hatred and let me sow love;
Reveal truth in the midst of my errors;
Pardon me for those I've injured;
In my doubting let faith permeate the fibers of my darkness;
For in the presence of my suffering, peace abounds.

O Divine Master,
Grant that I may not so much seek
To be consoled, as to console;
To be understood, as to understand;
To be forgiven, as to forgive;
To be loved as to love.

For it is in giving that I receive;
It is in pardoning that I'm pardoned;
And it is in my death to self that I have life and life more abundantly. Amen.

Silent Meditation

**Please rise in body and/or spirit.*

Meditation

I love God, whoever he is, and I'd really like to get closer to him. I've been thinking about how one of the simplest ways to get close to a woman is to be good to her children. To be kind and gentle and pay close attention to the things that make them special. To try to see her children the way she sees her children. And how God made us in his image. How he is the mother and father of all of us. So I wonder it that would be the best way to get closer to him too. By being kind and gentle to his children and noticing all the things that make them special. So many of us spend our time trying to find God in books, but maybe the simplest way to God is directly through the hearts of his children.

GLENNON MELTON, *CARRY ON, WARRIOR*

PRAYERS OF THE PEOPLE

Prayer Response Every Time I Feel the Spirit *African American Spiritual*

Every time I feel the Spirit moving in my heart I will pray.
Yes, every time I feel the Spirit moving in my heart I will pray.

Lord's Prayer

Our Father, who art in heaven, hallowed be Thy name.
Thy kingdom come, Thy will be done, on earth as it is in heaven.
Give us this day our daily bread,
And forgive us our debts, as we forgive our debtors.
And lead us not into temptation, but deliver us from evil.
For Thine is the kingdom, and the power, and the glory, forever. Amen.

A TIME OF GIFTS AND OFFERINGS

Invitation to the Offering

Offertory Now Thank We All Our God *Tune: NUN DANKET*
Resounding Joy Handbell Choir
Marcus Mack, director

***Offertory Response** What a Mighty God We Serve *Traditional African Folk Song*

What a mighty God we serve.
What a mighty God we serve.
Angels bow before You,
Heaven and earth adore You,
What a mighty God we serve.

Blessing of the Offering

BAPTISM (11:00)

***HYMN #459** Come, O Fount of Every Blessing

***BENEDICTION**

POSTLUDE Praise Him! Praise Him! *Tune: JOYFUL SONG, arr. Mark Hayes*

You are invited to exit Duhamel Hall quietly, or remain seated during the musical postlude, to enjoy a last moment of worship.

Assurance of Grace

Sung Response I've Got Peace Like a River *African American Spiritual*

I've got peace like a river,
I've got peace like a river,
I've got peace like a river in my soul.

ANTHEM (11:00) Come by Here *African American Spiritual, arr. Stephen Lee*

THE WORD OF GOD Matthew 5:38-48

You have heard that it was said, "An eye for an eye and a tooth for a tooth." But I say to you, Do not resist an evildoer. But if anyone strikes you on the right cheek, turn the other also; and if anyone wants to sue you and take your coat, give your cloak as well; and if anyone forces you to go one mile, go also the second mile. Give to everyone who begs from you, and do not refuse anyone who wants to borrow from you.

You have heard that it was said, "You shall love your neighbor and hate your enemy." But I say to you, Love your enemies and pray for those who persecute you, so that you may be children of your Parent in heaven, who makes the sun rise on the evil and on the good, and sends rain on the righteous and on the unrighteous. For if you love those who love you, what reward do you have? Do not even the tax collectors do the same? And if you greet only your brothers and sisters and siblings, what more are you doing than others? Do not even the Gentiles do the same? Be perfect, therefore, as your heavenly Parent is perfect. (*New Revised Standard Version*, alt.)

Silence

READER: In the beginning was the Word,
ALL: And the Word was with God.

SERMON Big Love Rev. Molly Baskette

***HYMN #396** Where Charity and Love Prevail

FIRST THINGS: LIFE IN OUR COMMUNITY

THIS WEEK AT FIRST CHURCH SOMERVILLE

Sunday, February 23

9a Worship and Church School
Rev. Molly Baskette, preaching
10a Coffee Hour
10a Adult and Children's Choir Rehearsal
11a Worship — Rev. Molly Baskette, preaching
12:30p Resounding Joy Rehearsal

Monday, February 24

5p Project SOUP

Wednesday, February 26

8:30a Visit with Molly at Diesel Café
7p Knit & Purl

Thursday, February 27

8:30a Visit with Jeff at Diesel Café

Friday, February 28

6:30p Lindy Bomb Squad

Sunday, March 2

9a Worship, Communion, and Church School
Rev. Molly Baskette, preaching
10a Coffee Hour
10a Adult and Children's Choir Rehearsal
11a Worship and Communion
Rev. Molly Baskette, preaching
12:30p Resounding Joy Rehearsal

89 College Avenue, Somerville, MA 02144
(617) 625-6485 - OFFICE@FIRSTCHURCHSOMERVILLE.ORG
WWW.FIRSTCHURCHSOMERVILLE.ORG
Rev. Molly Baskette: mbaskette@firstchurchsomerville.org
Rev. Jeff Mansfield: jmansfield@firstchurchsomerville.org

LEAD PASTOR
Rev. Molly Baskette

ASSOCIATE PASTOR
Rev. Jeffrey Mansfield

MUSIC DIRECTOR AND ORGANIST
Hugh Hinton

ASSISTANT MUSIC DIRECTOR
Marcus Mack

DIRECTOR OF FAMILY MINISTRY
Melissa Hines Shungu

SUNDAY SCHOOL
Melissa Hogle
Chelsey Valentine
Christy Zuzelo

NURSERY
Meghana Agni

MODERATOR
Gianna Marzilli Ericson

SENIOR DEACONS
Heather May
Pete Shungu
Jenny Utech

COMMUNITY MINISTERS
Rev. Diane Christopherson
Rev. Jason Donnelly
Rev. Reebee Kavich Girash
Rev. Kerrie Harthan
Rev. James Matarazzo
Rev. Carol Taylor
Rev. Laura Tuach
Rev. Jeff VonWald

CUSTODIAN
Blanca Portillo Peña

ADMINISTRATOR
Carol Luongo